1008278911

Conducting Undergraduate Research in Education

This book offers a student-focused guide to conducting undergraduate research in education and education-related programs, engaging students in the process of learning through research, and supporting them to navigate their multidimensional academic programs.

Written for undergraduate students in teacher education programs, the book features a range of leading voices in the field who offer a step-by-step guide to all elements of the research process: from conducting a literature review and choosing a research topic, to collecting data and building a research community with peers and mentors. Ultimately, volume editors Ruth J. Palmer and Deborah L. Thompson help model the competencies that students need to succeed, including complex thinking, strategic design, modeling, and persistent iterative practice, while demonstrating how conducting research can help students develop as deep thinkers, courageous researchers, and active participants in their communities of practice.

Offering strategic approaches, support, and guidance, this book demonstrates the wider importance of undergraduate research in informing educational practice and policy, as well as understanding schools beyond the classroom context, encouraging active engagement and continued learning progression.

Ruth J. Palmer is Emeritus Professor at The College of New Jersey where, as an Educational Psychologist with a teaching/research focus on adolescence, she was a member of the Department of Educational Administration and Secondary Education in the School of Education, and Affiliate Professor in the Department of African American Studies.

Deborah L. Thompson is Emeritus Professor at The College of New Jersey where she was a member of the Department of Elementary and Early Childhood Education. She taught graduate and undergraduate courses in literacy and children's literature. She also served as an adjunct professor in the Department of Women's, Gender and Sexuality Studies where she taught a course on gender in children's literature.

Routledge Undergraduate Research Series

Series Editors: *Gregory Young, Montana State University, and Jenny Olin Shanahan, Bridgewater State University*

Undergraduate Research in Music
A Guide for Students
Gregory Young and Jenny Olin Shanahan

Undergraduate Research in Art
A Guide for Students
Vaughan Judge, Jenny Olin Shanahan, and Gregory Young

Undergraduate Research in Dance
A Guide for Students
Lynnette Young Overby, Jenny Olin Shanahan, and Gregory Young

Undergraduate Research in Film
A Guide for Students
Lucia Ricciardelli, Jenny Olin Shanahan, and Gregory Young

Undergraduate Research in Architecture
A Guide for Students
D. Andrew Vernooy, Jenny Olin Shanahan, and Gregory Young

Undergraduate Research in History
A Guide for Students
Molly Todd, Jenny Olin Shanahan, and Gregory Young

Conducting Undergraduate Research in Education
A Guide for Students in Teacher Education Programs
Edited by Ruth J. Palmer and Deborah L. Thompson

https://www.routledge.com/Routledge-Undergraduate-Research-Series/book-series/RURS

Conducting Undergraduate Research in Education

A Guide for Students in Teacher Education Programs

**Edited by
Ruth J. Palmer and
Deborah L. Thompson**

Routledge
Taylor & Francis Group

NEW YORK AND LONDON

Cover image: © Getty Images

First published 2022
by Routledge
605 Third Avenue, New York, NY 10158

and by Routledge
2 Park Square, Milton Park, Abingdon, Oxon, OX14 4RN

Routledge is an imprint of the Taylor & Francis Group, an informa business

© 2022 selection and editorial matter, Ruth J. Palmer and Deborah L. Thompson; individual chapters, the contributors

The right of Ruth J. Palmer and Deborah L. Thompson to be identified as the authors of the editorial material, and of the authors for their individual chapters, has been asserted in accordance with sections 77 and 78 of the Copyright, Designs and Patents Act 1988.

Library of Congress Cataloging-in-Publication Data
Names: Palmer, Ruth J., editor. | Thompson, Deborah L., editor.
Title: Conducting undergraduate research in education : a guide for students in teacher education programs / edited by Ruth J. Palmer and Deborah L. Thompson.
Description: New York, NY : Routledge, 2022. | Includes bibliographical references and index.
Identifiers: LCCN 2021042465 | ISBN 9781032128535 (hardback) | ISBN 9781032128368 (paperback) | ISBN 9781003226475 (ebook)
Subjects: LCSH: Education—Research—Methodology.
Classification: LCC LB1028 .C583 2022 | DDC 370.72—dc23/
eng/20211203
LC record available at https://lccn.loc.gov/2021042465

ISBN: 978-1-032-12853-5 (hbk)
ISBN: 978-1-032-12836-8 (pbk)
ISBN: 978-1-003-22647-5 (ebk)

DOI: 10.4324/9781003226475

Typeset in Bembo
by codeMantra

Contents

Figures

Tables

Contributors

Judi Puritz Cook, PhD, is an affiliated faculty member at The College of New Jersey (TCNJ), where she also serves as director of the Office of Instructional Design. Her research focuses on the intersection of media and technology, with an emphasis on emerging media and commercial culture. She also develops digital pedagogy resources for faculty who teach in blended and online environments. Prior to working at TCNJ, Cook served as a professor in the media and communication department at Salem State University for 16 years.

Jody Eberly, EdD, is a professor of early childhood education in the Department of Elementary and Early Childhood Education at The College of New Jersey. She teaches undergraduate and graduate classes in early childhood curriculum, early and emergent literacy, child development, and multicultural children's literature. She earned her doctorate in elementary and early childhood education with an emphasis in early childhood education from Rutgers University. Her research interests include culturally responsive pedagogy, teacher dispositions toward culture, and children's play.

Arti Joshi, PhD, is professor and coordinator of the elementary program in the Department of Elementary and Early Childhood Education at The College of New Jersey. She earned her PhD in child and family studies at Syracuse University. She teaches foundation courses at the undergraduate and graduate levels. Her research focuses on cultural diversity in the context of educational settings, home–school relations, and teacher preparation programs; one area of her research focus has been working with Asian Indian families. She also serves as a member of the National Advisory Board for the *School and Community Journal*. Besides teaching, she enjoys music, art, world cinema, and reading fiction books with global themes.

Suzanne F. Lindt, PhD, is an associate professor in the Department of Curriculum and Learning at Midwestern State University in Texas. As a faculty member in education, she is passionate about research and the importance of providing the next generation of teachers with the tools needed to conduct research in their future classrooms and schools. She has worked with 15 undergraduate students on diverse individual research projects, including those on assessment in social studies, engagement in science, self-concept development in gifted learners, and formative assessment with technology.

Giang-Nguyen T. Nguyen, PhD, is an associate professor of mathematics education in the Department of Teacher Education and Educational Leadership at the University of West Florida. Her research focuses on factors that influence an individual's motivation for learning and teaching mathematics and helping teachers develop their mathematical knowledge as well as the pedagogical content knowledge for teaching mathematics. She has taught undergraduate and graduate courses in mathematics education, research design, field experience, technology in teaching mathematics. In addition, she has served as a member of the IRB (Institutional Review Board) for the past eight years.

Catherine L. Packer-Williams, PhD, is a counseling psychologist and an American Psychological Association (APA) Substance Abuse and Mental Health Services Administration Minority Fellow, with 20 years of experience in education, from K-12 through higher education. She has been an elementary education teacher, school counselor program coordinator, professor of counselor education, dean of instruction, and accreditation liaison in the Alabama community college system. Her research focuses on the intersections of gender, race, counseling/psychology, and education and has contributed to the literature related to the experiences of African American women in the academy, particularly regarding mentoring, professional identity, and psychological well-being.

Ruth J. Palmer, PhD, is professor emerita of The College of New Jersey where, as an educational psychologist, she was a member of the Department of Educational Administration and Secondary Education in the School of Education, and affiliate professor in the Department of African American Studies. Her teaching foci included adolescent psychology and research methods; she also served as faculty in the first-year seminars where she focused on student leadership generally and in teacher education. Her scholarship included mentored undergraduate research, faculty-student collaboration, and teacher identity. She demonstrated her leadership capacity as research fellow in the Office of the Dean, 2018–2019, a two-term Ewing Township School Board member, a co-founder of the Council on Undergraduate Research (CUR) Education Division, a member of CUR's Executive Board (2018–2020), and CUR's president -elect (2021–2022).

Emily N. Smith, EdD, is an assistant professor in the Department of Special Education at Midwestern State University in Wichita Falls,

Texas. She assists undergraduate students in developing an understanding of published works, determining their areas of research interest, and cultivating a passion for research. She has worked with ten undergraduate students on individual research projects, on topics including reading fluency, math fluency, classroom observations, ADD and college students, Tourette Syndrome, transition, and movement in the classroom.

Carla J. Thompson, EdD, is professor of educational research and administration for the University of West Florida (UWF) and has served as Chair of UWF's Institutional Review Board for the past ten years. She has published more than 50 articles and conference papers on research ethics and educational research; she received a grant from the U.S. Office of Research Integrity (2017) devoted to research integrity and sensitive populations. She teaches research methods and ethics for the UWF EdD program and directs the UWF Community Outreach Research and Learning (CORAL) Center within the College of Education.

Deborah L. Thompson, PhD, is professor emerita at the College of New Jersey. During her tenure in higher education, she taught graduate and undergraduate literacy and children's literature courses. Her recent works include a comparative analysis of Cinderella's tales from the African diaspora and a chapter on current trends in nonfiction literature for children. She is a member of the Council on Undergraduate Research (CUR) Education Division.

Sylvia Tiala, PhD, is a tenured professor and director of the Nakatani Teaching and Learning Center (NTLC) at the University of Wisconsin-Stout. The NTLC provides professional development programming for faculty and academic instructional staff with the goal to build confidence and effectiveness of instructors' teaching practices. She came to the position after 14 years of teaching undergraduate- and graduate-level courses in face-to-face, online, and blended environments for UW-Stout's teaching, learning, and leadership department. She is passionate about embedding research into the courses she teaches, including through students' independent research projects, mentoring McNair scholars, and embedding whole-class research projects into courses related to education, game design, and teacher preparation. She also serves as committee chair and research advisor for students enrolled in master's and doctoral programs. She leads sharing communities and presents nationally and internationally on utilizing Willison and O'Regan's (2007) *Research Skill Development Framework*.

Preface

Undergraduate research in teacher education programs is a critical component of the transformation of teaching and learning in higher education. Along with other high-impact practices in undergraduate education, undergraduate research has become the standard in the enterprise of knowledge building, student-engaged learning, and prospective teachers' proposed professional practice. Yet, although foundational work has been accomplished, in terms of initiating undergraduate research into teacher education programs, its full adoption has not yet been realized across all schools and colleges of education. In designing this text, we argue that elements of this transformation in teacher education programs can originate in the work of its major stakeholders: undergraduate students enrolled in teacher education programs.

This book, then, with its focus on the research processes, targets undergraduate students in teacher education programs; they are already invested in their professional choices and in their chosen institutions. By engaging these students in the processes of learning through research, we aim to help them uncover and navigate learning pathways to and through their multidimensional academic programs. Therefore, this book has been planned and proposed to provide targeted support and guidance to students and their mentors in teacher education programs, relative to the conduct of undergraduate research and its applications inside and outside of the classroom. Its objectives are to

- present an organized and resourceful text focused on students' active engagement and their continuing learning progression toward the ethical conduct of undergraduate research;
- provide precise support and strategic approaches to undergraduate research that serve to build capacity for self-directed and productive engagement in the research practices related to the myriad areas of study in teacher education;
- underscore the proven short- and long-term benefits of adopting the practice of undergraduate research (e.g., building transferable skills, developing leadership capacity and self-advocacy, and contributing knowledge to one's professional field) and guide students to recognize

emergent benefits in areas of academic emotions, professional dispositions, and mindful commitment to peer collaboration and mentoring;

- introduce the works of educational giants whose contributions provide students a rich legacy of conceptual/complex thinking, inter- and
multi-disciplinary research, and high-quality professional practice.
This approach helps students define and redefine their teaching self/
identity and activate their capacity to contribute to a culture of inquiry in their undergraduate classrooms and those in K-12 schools.

Accordingly, this book provides a valuable and effective tool that serves to
fully engage students in teacher education programs in all elements of the
research process. In addition, it aims to facilitate the emergence of cadres
of teachers who can translate the research process into a thinking routine
to address any challenge or dilemma in their future professional practice.

The book's basic design rests on the rich contributions of national and
international scholarly investigators and of educational practitioners who
populate the extensive fields of education research. That basic design is
enriched by the adoption of approaches to undergraduate research in education from intersecting perspectives, including (a) the interdisciplinary
and complex field of education, (b) teacher/educator learning and leadership as identity learning, and (c) "students as partners" in teaching and
learning. These themes are threaded subtly through the chapters, allowing
students to reach beyond their acknowledged capacities into more complex thinking and reasoned action, to which students in teacher education
programs aspire.

Introducing the Text

As editors, we were intentional in the organization of the chapters; while
the initial focus was on appropriate sequencing of chapters specifically related to the research process, we also strove to intersperse among those (a)
chapters that support specific tasks, (b) those that support the ever-present
academic emotions and other learning dispositions, and (c) those that urge
the building of a sustainability plan, beginning with extending the practice of research beyond the classroom.

The first chapter lays the foundation for the text; it offers students in
teacher education an opportunity first to locate themselves at a historical point in the evolution of undergraduate education, when there was a
national call to higher education institutions to establish research-based
learning as its standard, and in tandem, a call to professional schools to
provide the same inquiry-based opportunities to their students. Then
Chapter 1 appeals to students to be attentive to the research-related promises and benefits offered by their higher education institution and to invest themselves in ways necessary to attain those benefits and anticipated
outcomes. The goal at the beginning of this text is to elevate the power

of institutional pride and personal/professional identity as fundamental motivating factors, first for engagement in research-related initiatives in teacher education programs, and second for assuming the role of responsible bearers of the message to peers and their K-12 students.

We then present the core chapters. Chapter 2 is an introduction to the research question as the central element of the research process; it is followed by Chapter 3, about the review of the literature. After these we place Chapter 4, "The Demands of Reading, Writing, and Thinking Like Researchers," and Chapter 5, "Technology: The All-Purpose Research Tool for Discovery, Organization, and Collaboration." These chapters support the initial tasks: one related to the core competencies of reading, writing, and thinking (like a researcher) and the other focused on technological tools of research.

The text then lays out the next steps in the research process. Chapter 6 describes and explains the tasks of narrowing the topic, designing the methods, and conducting research ethically. Chapter 7 addresses analyzing data. Next we inserted Chapter 8, "Building Your Research Community with Peers, Near-peers, and Mentors," to remind students that learning is a social activity and that collaborative work is a benchmark of the research environment, especially in the early years of involvement in the experience. Chapter 8 provides students in teacher education programs with iterative steps to actively seek out and engage in collaborations and partnerships with faculty and peers to advance their work.

Chapters 9 and 10 together serve to guide the report-writing process. Chapter 9 helps student-researchers in teacher education programs to understand the results of their data analysis and to discern and communicate their meaning. Chapter 10 focuses on a most important part of the research process: disseminating the results and findings to multiple communities. The emphasis is on communications and future action.

Chapter 11 urges students to take their research-related learning beyond the classroom and, in the process, to activate the practice of self-directed learning and learner agency. For students in teacher education programs, the goal is to maximize their learner potential related to the application of research-related capacities; this they can do in their communities of practice.

It is our expectation that this text can accomplish the goals set by all the contributing authors and contribute to students' success in the specific research-related tasks in and beyond the classroom. More importantly, we hope that in using this text to support their research experiences students can progress successfully through their academic programs.

Ruth J. Palmer, Editor
Deborah L. Thompson, Editor

Acknowledgments

This work has had a long germination period. To all who supported us on the journey, many thanks, especially the councilors of the CUR Education Division who demonstrated early support for the project and authored selected chapters. Furthermore, we proudly recognize one of our chapter authors, a former undergraduate who participated in one of our earliest course-embedded research experiences. She continued her personal research path after graduating and enrolled in and successfully completed a research-focused doctoral program. We would be remiss, though, if we did not highlight those who remain to this day the inspiration for writing this book: our inquiring students, a formidable and persuasive advocate, a committed mentor, and a diligent role model.

First, we are grateful to the students in the teacher education programs in the institution in which we taught. Their desire to conduct research within the confines of a structured and sometimes inflexible set of course requirements never wavered. They conducted research-based independent studies on campus and during their study abroad experiences. They participated in summer research opportunities and found ways to turn course-embedded assignments into sterling pieces of research that they proudly presented at the campus-wide student achievement days, as well as at state, regional, and national conferences. They had papers published in peer-reviewed journals. Several presented at the American Educational Research Association (AERA)—the premiere educational research conference in the country. Undergraduate research opened avenues to students who had entered their teacher education programs with some sense of their vocational direction, but they wanted more from their major areas of study than how to write perfect lesson plans. Undergraduate research provided a pathway for teacher education majors to truly grasp how students learned. As one sophomore excitedly proclaimed after listening to a guest speaker on one of the School of Education's Undergraduate Research Days (more than 90 undergraduates attended this particular event without prodding or the promise of refreshments): "I didn't know we could do research in our education majors! I am going to do research until I graduate." And she did, as did many others.

Second, our formidable and intrepid advocate remains Dr. Sarah Kern, Faculty Emerita, The College of New Jersey, and former chairperson of the elementary and early childhood education department in the School of Education. She persuaded every faculty member in the department to participate in faculty-student scholarly collaboration in course-based research experiences. No faculty meeting, no departmental newsletter or communique went out without some mention of undergraduate research. She also reached across departments to support the work. Dr. Kern's devotion to undergraduate research was the incentive for the department to begin the work of identifying the course redesigns necessary to embed research in every undergraduate elementary and early childhood education course.

Next, we are grateful for the Council on Undergraduate Research (CUR) who after our participation in one of its institutes in 2010 provided us with a mentor, Dr. Andrea Chapdelaine, then provost at Albright College and now president of Hood College. For many years, she provided guidance not only about *learning through research* but also about providing collaborative leadership for our colleagues and for a school community effort. We appreciate the mentoring, the friendship, and her continued work with us in undergraduate research.

Finally, we thank our gifted mentor and campus role model, Dr. Jeffrey Osborne, then dean of the School of Science and now provost at The College of New Jersey, and one of the co-principal investigators of the CUR Curriculum Transformations Grant awarded by the National Science Foundation (NSF). We could not have made the progress in the early days of building an undergraduate research presence in the School of Education (SOE) were it not for Dr. Osborne. He shared with us and the SOE faculty his boundless expertise on undergraduate research. Dr. Osborne did not see undergraduate research as a tool of the sciences only; he believed that undergraduate research belonged in all disciplines of study. His participation in our Brown Bag Lecture Series provided us with a solid foundation for building an active and effective undergraduate research program in our teacher education programs. Dr. Osborne, thank you; we will always remain indebted to you.

Ruth J. Palmer, Editor
Deborah L. Thompson, Editor

Series Foreword

The Routledge Undergraduate Research Series was created to guide students and faculty through a wide variety of research and creative projects in diverse fields of study. Originally dedicated to undergraduate research in the fine and performing arts, the series has expanded to include programs in the humanities and education. Although academic disciplines outside the natural, physical, and social sciences have been underrepresented in many college and university research opportunities for undergraduate students, the global movement to expand access to undergraduate research is highly relevant to and powerfully transformational for students of all majors and programs. Each book in the series lays out stages of the research process in a particular discipline, with timely and applicable examples that illustrate common questions, considerations, and methods of scholars in the field. Chapter by chapter, the books show recursive and adaptable means of engaging in meaningful scholarship in the curriculum and co-curricularly. The books are written for undergraduates as well as faculty, staff, and graduate-student mentors with varying levels of research and mentoring experience.

Gregory Young and Jenny Olin Shanahan

1 Undergraduate Research in Teacher Education

The Legacy, the Promise, the Responsibility

Ruth J. Palmer

For decades, curriculum change in higher education has been simply additive—a new course, a new program, a new school, a new initiative, and so on. However, in 1998, there was a radical shift away from this approach: a call for curriculum change in higher education situated in a more extensive and transformational change process, institutional change. The Boyer Commission on Educating Undergraduates in the Research University published *Reinventing Undergraduate Education: A Blueprint for America's Research Universities* delivered this call for change and itemized the steps necessary for its implementation. Although the Commission may have just had research universities in mind, its recommendations remain guideposts for what should be done for undergraduates in all higher education institutions.

Consequently, the practice of undergraduate research has expanded rapidly across schools and programs, beginning in the sciences, but with a slower progression in professional schools including schools of education. Despite the slow pace of adoption, many undergraduates entering teacher education programs today have research expectations because they had opportunities to conduct research while in high school (Puri, 2017). Furthermore, the Boyer Commission Report stated emphatically that research opportunities are not only for students interested in science but also for students across all disciplines and programs. Twenty years after the 1998 benchmark report, many researchers, including Hensel (2018), reiterated that "research-based learning at the highest level is an ethical and moral imperative for all students in all disciplines across all their years of undergraduate education and beyond" (p. 12).

Purpose

Thus, this introductory chapter aims first to engage undergraduate teacher education students in thoughtful deliberations on the conduct of undergraduate research as proposed in the Boyer (1998) Commission Report on undergraduate education. The chapter focuses on specific recommendations from the Boyer Commission Report, that both address undergraduate education and has direct implications for teacher education programs. It then describes and analyzes selected higher education institutions'

DOI: 10.4324/9781003226475-1

responses to the recommendations and the application of those responses in schools of education. Subsequently, an invitation is extended to students to analyze and adopt currently available practices and assume those responsibilities related to the adoption of this educational legacy/change and the relevant institutional and disciplinary/professional actions/strategic plans on behalf of their undergraduate teacher education programs.

The overarching goal is to ensure that, with basic knowledge of the plan for the transformation of undergraduate education, students in teacher education program can target academic outcomes relative to this legacy of research-based learning and to an envisioning of an integrated personal/professional identity as teacher-instructor, complex thinker, and researcher in education, an interdisciplinary field. Introducing the subsequent chapters reveals secure and dependable steppingstones leading to a well-articulated student researcher skill development process.

Revisiting the Recommendations of Boyer Commission (1998), a Benchmark Document

At the center of the Boyer Commission Report are the following ten recommendations, initially made to higher education research institutions yet applied to all higher education institutions: (1) make research-based learning the standard, (2) construct an inquiry-based freshman year, (3) build on the freshman foundation, (4) remove barriers to interdisciplinary education, (5) link communication skills and course work, (6) use information technology creatively, (7) culminate with a capstone experience, (8) educate graduate students as apprentice teachers, (9) change faculty reward systems, and (10) cultivate a sense of community. For each of these, the report provided specific sub-recommendations, in addition to examples of applications in its targeted institutions. In the report's conclusion, the Commission reminded institutions that "their students, properly educated for the new millennium, will be required as leaders while that world continues to transform itself." This work reiterates the position that students must be informed about and actively engaged in this change process.

Thus, this section engages undergraduate teacher education students in this reflective journey. The focus here is on Recommendations 1, 4, and then 3 and 7 combined.

Recommendation I. Make Research-Based Learning the Standard

Undergraduate education in [research] universities, requires renewed emphasis on a point strongly made by John Dewey almost a century ago: learning is based on discovery guided by mentoring rather than on the transmission of information. Inherent in inquiry-based learning is an element of reciprocity: faculty can learn from students as students are learning from faculty.

Students in teacher education programs in accredited colleges and universities are now part of an international movement to educate capable, informed teacher-learners for service in changing K-12 schools, now and for an uncertain future; they are also expected to respond to, participate in, and provide solutions for local, national, and global challenges (pandemics, war, political upheavals, social injustices, etc.) that require an interdisciplinary approach. To achieve those competences, the recommended learning approach is learning *through* research and *for* discovery, an approach that surpasses rote learning and toolkits devoid of conceptual groundings, historical anchors, and/or contextual information. The endorsed approach of learning *through* research and *for* discovery remains to today an expectation for all institutions of higher education, including professional schools; prospective teachers as undergraduate students and learners are to be provided the same inquiry-based opportunities as students in research universities, particularly in the early college years. The Boyer Commission Report moves access to high-quality research and inquiry to the center of the undergraduate academic experience and advocating it for all students. This radical shift is unparalleled (Hensel, 2018).

The Boyer Commission emphasizes the reciprocal yet unwritten commitment between colleges/universities and enrolled students in which each assumes obligations and responsibilities and each receives benefits: (a) "By admitting a student, any college or university commits itself to provide maximal opportunities for intellectual and creative development [… and] opportunities to learn through inquiry rather than simple transmission of knowledge; and (b) the student commits to a course of study intended to lead to a degree, agrees to follow such rules of civil behavior as the university prescribes, accepts the challenge of making an appropriate contribution to the community of scholars, and *pledges to cultivate her or his mind, abilities, and talents with a view to becoming a productive and responsible citizen*" (pp. 12–13). These are part of the legacy of change in education, to which institutions and students are still expected to respond.

Institutional Responses and Enactments in Teacher Education Programs

Since 1998, the response to transform teaching and learning radically through research has grown exponentially across some fields of study and some academic and professional schools (Crawford & Shanahan, 2014; Małachowski, 2019). This has been supported by Kuh's (2008) submission of research as one of ten high-impact practices that have been incorporated in the design of signature experiences for undergraduate education. Institutions overall have supported learning through research, leaving it for the disciplines to develop and implement practices relevant to the discipline and programs. However, despite the clear evidence that research experiences constitute to a significant portion of the intellectual and practical skills essential for all undergraduate students, its full adoption remains uneven across schools of education (Table 1.1).

But it is important that undergraduate students in teacher education program comprehend the advocacy roles that their institutions, faculty, national associations, and international organizations assume on their behalf. Faculty have moved beyond just supporting faculty-initiated/ student-initiated studies and now design course-integrated research experiences through which student teachers gain access to learning through research and for discovery. Institutions have initiated annual events for students to showcase their work, for example, the one-day Celebration of Student Achievement, and the college-wide summer research programs and the launching of student journals.

Nationally, the honor society for Education Kappa Delta Pi (KDP) sponsors research activities within their local chapters and so does Phi Kappa Phi (PKP). In addition, America's premier educational research association— American Educational Research Association (AERA)—has incorporated special interest groups (SIGs) that focus on teacher research and on undergraduate research. So too has the American Association of Colleges of Teacher Education (AACTE) whose topical action groups (TAGs) conduct research in teacher education. More recently, the Association for Teacher Education (ATE) has launched an official student research group. The state chapters of the National Association for Multicultural Education (NAME) open membership to students with the mentors. Other educational organizations continue this advocacy for students in teacher education.

At the national and international levels, advocacy for undergraduate research has been the sole purpose of the Council for Undergraduate Research (CUR) of the United States, the British Council for

Table 1.1 Boyer Commission Recommendation I (Boyer Commission, 1998) and Institutional Responses

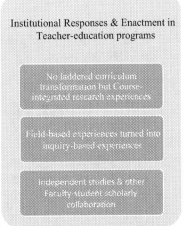

Recommendations to Higher Education

Institutional Responses & Enactment in Teacher-education programs

No laddered curriculum transformation but Course-integrated research experiences

Make Research-based Learning the Standard

Field-based experiences turned into inquiry-based experiences

Independent studies & other Faculty-student scholarly collaboration

Undergraduate Research (BCUR), the Australasian Council of Undergraduate Research (ACUR), and other affiliates. These organizations support student research in teacher education programs, and their annual meetings are reminders to student teachers that there are groups and individuals who are working on their behalf to ensure a clear and emphatic response to the call for research-based learning as the standard for the transformation of undergraduate education and, by implication, the transformation of teacher education.

Student Responsibilities and the Benefits of Research-Related Learning

It is important that students in teacher education programs attain membership in these and other professional organizations at some point in their academic careers; local chapters and special programs offer them the opportunity to extend gratitude to those who advocate on their behalf and to collaborate with peers and near-peers in the undergraduate research effort.

Within these organizations and in their programs, students can initiate student-type advocacy actions (Nishino, 2012), for example, (a) identify and enroll in courses that provide course-embedded research experiences; (b) volunteer-designated research-learning hours in faculty-led research activities; (c) reflective journaling in early field placements/practica and in student teaching your field placements/practica/internships (Palmer, 2015); (d) submitting projects/assignments papers, posters, art exhibitions, video discussions, and other products of student work to the college's symposium or celebration of student achievement; (e) starting a study group to master the academic literature and to practice the synthesis of information. These activities reinforce skills and competencies and serve to support classroom learning and participation.

However, there are additional efforts being made for undergraduate students in teacher education programs. At the program level, while students are recruited to work on faculty-initiated research, faculty are also (a) revising their courses to offer course-based inquiry experiences, (b) restructuring their field placements to ensure applied learning experiences, and (c) translating classroom learning into structured community-based learning. It is important that these efforts become transparent to students, who in turn can then respond with their own determination to realize the substantial benefits:

- Skills they need to become conscientious, purposeful, and effective professional educators (Manak & Young, 2014).
- Personal and professional gains as emerging researchers (Lopatto, 2007).
- Proficiency in applying the research process in problem-solving and inquiry (Nolan et al., 2020).

- Self-confidence, clarification of a career path, and eagerness to engage in more challenging research activities (Palmer et al., 2015).
- Resilience and tolerance for complex issues (Crowe & Boe, 2019).

Altogether, when students in teacher education programs understand the legacy of their field and acknowledge the role that their institutions and other organizations play to ensure access to that rich inheritance—learning through research and for discovery is the standard—they themselves can confidently manage their engagement and their future.

Recommendation IV: Remove Barriers to Interdisciplinary Research

> [Research]universities must remove barriers to and create mechanisms for much more interdisciplinary undergraduate education.

Students in teacher education programs embrace their program as situated in, and impacted by, all the characteristics of the broader interdisciplinary field of education. Interdisciplinary fields of study like education rely on shared knowledge from across disciplines, integrating that knowledge into a coordinated, interactive, and coherent whole (Mason, 2008; Miller, 2020).

Interdisciplinarity as a construct/concept, a practice, and a field has had an embattled history; its conceptualization, application, and implementations have had both advocates and detractors (Bernini & Woods, 2014). However, interdisciplinarity's embattled history does not negate its contribution to higher education and to the field of education. Arneback and Blåsjö (2017) and Oliveira Medeiros (2015) underscore the capacity of interdisciplinarity to

a   challenge students' cognitive and social-emotional capacities through systems thinking, knowledge integration, transfer of knowledge, analysis of multifaceted issues, synthesizing, and perspective taking.
b   enrich students' lifelong learning habits and academic skills.
c   enhance students' personal growth in the exploration of topics across a range of subject boundaries;
d   motivate students to pursue new knowledge across different subject areas.
    Interestingly, these are the competencies to which students in teacher education programs aspire, with research-related learning as the means to that end.

In sum, the interdisciplinary characteristics of the field of education/ teacher education constitute the context, the first layer of study in relation to undergraduate research. Students along with faculty are expected to immerse themselves in interdisciplinarity, to make transparent its complex systems and to uncover order, patterns, and structures that arise from those systems. Such immersion sheds light on the place and practice of undergraduate research (Arneback & Blåsjö, 2017).

Removal of Barriers to Interdisciplinarity: Institutional Response and Enactments in Teacher Education Programs

In recent decades, multiple national and international organization and institutions have acknowledged and advocated for interdisciplinary research defined in varying ways across groups. However, the following confirms what they all agree on:

> [Interdisciplinary research is] ... a mode of research by teams/individuals that integrates information, data, techniques, tools, perspectives, concepts, and/or theories from two or more disciplines or bodies of specialized knowledge to advance fundamental understanding or to solve problems whose solutions are beyond the scope of a single discipline or area of research practice.
>
> (Committee on Facilitating Interdisciplinary Research, Committee on Science, Engineering, and Public Policy, 2004)

Teacher education programs are filled with students from across multiple disciplines, available to engage in such work with their faculty mentors. Together they can build team capacity to address the complex and intersecting issues of teaching and learning in schools and in communities, for example, training interdisciplinary groups of tutors to serve middle and high school students. For some, opportunities may present themselves in their early program field placement or practicum; for more advanced students, more challenging opportunities emerge through their partnership with their mentors. Faculty grant work provides such opportunities; for example, the National Science Foundation (NSF) is one organization that promotes interdisciplinary research through its grant programs that support the development of the next generation of researchers. The support from these programs enhances the support for undergraduates, graduate students, and postdoctoral researchers generally. The organization's rationale is summarized as follows: Society's challenges are often complex and require an integrative, collaborative approach; these areas are often interdisciplinary. In sum, faculty mentors serve as supportive agents who provide information relative to research opportunities to students in teacher education programs. Effective mentoring is crucial to students' success; students' contribution include full participation, active and engaged learning, and continuing academic investment (Table 1.2).

Table 1.2 Boyer Commission Recommendation IV (Boyer Commission, 1998). Remove Barriers to Interdisciplinary and Institutional Responses

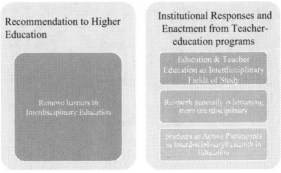

Removing Barriers to Interdisciplinarity: Students' Responsibilities and Benefits Relative to Interdisciplinarity

Learning through research in education means attention to the field and to teaching (in teacher education programs) as interdisciplinary and complex but not necessarily complicated. Bernini and Woods (2014) and Oliveira Medeiros (2015) indicate that the challenge and the promise for students in teacher education programs are for them to

• understand, embrace, value, and invest in the field of education and in their program of choice as interdisciplinary.
• demonstrate personal investment with an ethical commitment to integrate disciplinary and professional choice through mentored faculty-student scholarly collaboration.
• be active, engaged learners who integrate scholarly collaboration with other high-impact practices.
• focus on conceptual and theoretical learning as the platform for the practical, everyday actions related to becoming a teacher and educational leader.

Undergirding these recommendations is a call for students in teacher education programs to invest their academic assets in the interdisciplinary field of education through mentored undergraduate research. Students' scholarly collaboration with their mentors opens the doors to the complexity of interdisciplinarity.

Boyer Commission Report

Recommendation III: Build on the Freshman Foundation
Recommendation VII: Culminate with a Capstone Experience

The first year of a university experience needs to provide new stimulation for intellectual growth and a firm grounding in inquiry-based learning and communication of information and ideas.

The final semester(s) should focus on a major project and utilize to the fullest the research and communication skills learned in the previous semesters.

Together, these two recommendations clarify the intent of the Boyer Commission recommendations, which is the transformation of the higher education institutions' structure and delivery systems, including curricula, programs, faculty work, student life, and supporting services. For all students, and for undergraduate teacher education students in particular, the required transformation is about the transformation of students' entire academic experience—Year 1 through to graduation. The Boyer Commission conceptualized and anticipated student life not simply as an accumulation of classes (although those are important) but as a consciously threaded sequence of research and research-related experiences that transform students into complex thinkers, proficient in the Five Minds of the Future: disciplined, synthesizing, creating, respectful, and ethical (Gardner, 2006).

Institutional Responses and Enactments in Teacher Education Programs

Institutions have provided resources to support the achievement of these goals. Evidence to that effect include (a) long-range curricula transformation enhanced with digital technologies alongside more responsive advisement, a constellation of mentoring practices, plus, the infusion of

Table 1.3 Boyer Commission Recommendations III and VII (Boyer Commission, 1998) and Institutional Responses

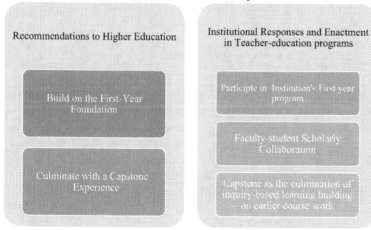

Recommendations to Higher Education	Institutional Responses and Enactment in Teacher-education programs
Build on the First-Year Foundation	Participate in Institution's First year program
	Faculty-student Scholarly Collaboration
Culminate with a Capstone Experience	Capstone as the culmination of inquiry-based learning building on earlier course work

extracurricular activities that provide clear indicators of community values and traditions. Institutions also invested in infrastructure upgrades, with the sole purpose of enhancing campus life, community-building, and safety (Table 1.3).

Benefits and Responsibilities—Undergraduate Students in Teacher Education Programs

Students in teacher education programs benefit from these enhancements. To these are added assignments and exercises redesigned to ensure the acquisition of research-related skills, for example, creativity, good judgment, communication, organization, and persistence—all equally important skills to make the leap from gaining knowledge from others' discoveries to making discoveries on your own (Showman, Cat, Cook, Holloway, & Wittman, 2013). These student authors add that these research-related skills are universally applicable in the pursuit of becoming a researcher and "provide a foundation for not only what it means to be an undergraduate researcher, but also to create the opportunity for a dialogue among researchers at all levels, from the undergraduate to the tenured professor, regarding what makes undergraduate researchers truly succeed" (p. 19). Altogether, the institutional enhancements and the research-related skills enhance the learning environment and reinforce the **institutional values**.

Students in teacher education programs with the assistance of their mentors are expected to learn how to recognize, navigate, and commit to full engagement in the opportunities designed to enable their personal strategic planning. Peer/near-peer study groups contribute to that capacity to extend learning beyond the classroom and to access resources on campus, in the community, and/or online. Such groups can help in terms of rehearsing ways to negotiate with faculty and/or staff regarding the direction and progress toward their academic goals (Brew & Saunders, 2020).

From Boyer to Navigating the Rich Terrain of Research in Teacher Education

The implementation of the recommendations of the Boyer Commission Report (1998) is in its 24th year; higher education institutions and their schools of education continue to translate the recommendations in the direction of a coherent curriculum that aligns with state and national accreditation standards for teaching. The lesson here is that change is a complex process over multiple phases and stages; Breen et al. (2003) and Brew and Saunders (2020) confirm the complexity of curriculum change.

Nevertheless, the previous sections aimed to make evident the call for change within the legacy of higher education, followed by responses/

promises in the strategic plans of institutions (schools and areas of study) and the responsibilities of individuals/stakeholders, specifically students. This chapter altogether alerts students specifically (as stakeholders in the teaching/learning experience) about their participation in and contribution to the change process in partnership with their peers and mentors; it also reminds students of Barbara Rogoff's (2003) guidance regarding human development and cultural processes: "humans develop through their changing participation in the socio-cultural activities of their communities which also change" (p. 11).

For students in schools of education, the challenge is to identify the interrelationship across legacy, promises, and individual responsible action. Participation in the research process enables that understanding and any effort to become complex thinkers who develop a *thinking routine* or *a habit of mind* to address spontaneously every complex issue, problem, and dilemma encountered. The Boyer Commission Recommendations (I, III, and VII) identify the dispositions the development of which parallel such achievements: autonomy, learner agency, and urgent deliberate action. When these are integrated with classroom learning, and the adoption of higher-level thinking skills, as in the case of the Models of Engaged Learning and Teaching (MELT; Willison & O'Regan, 2006; Willison, 2018), they promise success for student efforts.

Models of Engaged Learning and Teaching (MELT)

Willison (2018) introduced the MELT—a series of models that clarify for students the types of thinking needed for research skill development and for lifelong learning. Together, these models are tools to scaffold thinking skill development in such a way that MELT becomes a *thinking routine* for students. The first of the MELT models was the Research Skill Development (RSD) framework,[1] developed in 2006, which uses terminology/concepts/facets that reflect the research processes; it helps teachers to scaffold the skills associated with research and support students own skills development and self-monitoring and overall learner autonomy (Table 1.4).

Bandaranaike (2018) confirms that the cross-table format of the framework systematically maps the development of both students' research skills and their increasing levels of autonomy across a course or program of

---

1 Jabareen (2009): I define conceptual framework as a network, or "a plane," of interlinked concepts that together provide a comprehensive understanding of a phenomenon or phenomena. The concepts that constitute a conceptual framework support one another, articulate their respective phenomena, and establish a framework-specific philosophy.

Table 1.4 Research Skill Development (RSD) Framework

For educators to facilitate the explicit, coherent, incremental, and cyclic development of the skills associated with researching, problem-solving, critical thinking, and clinical reasoning.

	Students' Autonomy When Researching				
	Prescribed Researching	*Bounded Researching*	*Scaffolded Researching*	*Open-ended Researching*	*Unbounded Researching*
Students develop a research mindset through engagement with content and increasing awareness of ethical, cultural, social, and team (ECST) aspects, when they…	Highly structured directions and modelling from educator prompt researching, in which…	Boundaries set by and limited directions from educator channel researching, in which…	Scaffolds placed by educator shape independent researching, in which…	Students initiate research and this is guided by the educator…	Students-determined guidelines for researching that are in accord with discipline or context…
Curious **Embark and clarify** *What is our purpose?* Students respond to or initiate research and clarify what knowledge is required, considering ECST issues.	Students respond to questions/tasks arising explicitly from a closed inquiry. Use a provided structured approach to clarify questions, terms, requirements, expectations, and ECST issues.	Students respond to questions/t asks required by and implicit in a closed inquiry. Choose from several provided structures to clarify questions, terms, requirements, expectations, and ECST issues.	Students respond to questions/ tasks generated from a closed inquiry. Choose from a range of provided structures or approaches to clarify questions, requirements, Expectations, and ECST issues.	*Students generate questions /aims/ hypotheses framed within structured guidelines★.* Anticipate and prepare for ECST issues.	★*Students generate questions/aims/ questions/aims/ hypotheses based on experience, expertise, and literature★.* Delve into and prepare for ECST issues.

Find and generate *What do we need?* Students find and generate needed information/data using appropriate methodology.	Determined	Students collect and record required information/data using a prescribed methodology from a prescribed source in which the information/data is evident.	Students collect and record appropriate information/data using given methodology from predetermined source/s where information/data are not obvious.	Students collect and record appropriate information/data from self-selected sources using one of several provided methodologies.	Students collect and record self-determined information/data choosing an appropriate methodology based on parameters set.	Students collect and record information/data from self-selected sources, choosing or devising an appropriate methodology with self-structured guidelines.
Evaluate and reflect *What do we trust?* Students determine the credibility of sources, information, and data and make own research processes visible.	Discerning	Students evaluate sources/information/data using simple prescribed criteria to specify credibility and to reflect on the research process.	Students evaluate sources/information/data using a choice of provided criteria to specify credibility and to reflect on the research process.	Students evaluate sources/information/data and inquiry process using criteria related to the aims of the inquiry. Reflect insightfully to improve own processes used.	Students evaluate information/data and the inquiry process using self-determined criteria developed within parameters given. Reflects to refine others' processes.	Students evaluate information/data and inquiry process rigorously using self-generated criteria based on experience, expertise, and the literature. Reflect insightfully to renew others' processes.
Organize and manage *How do we arrange?* Students organize information and data to reveal patterns/themes, managing teams, and processes.	Harmonizing	Students organize information/data using prescribed structure. Manage linear process provided (with prespecified team roles).	Students organize information/data using a choice of given structures. Manage a process that has alternative possible pathways (and specify team roles).	Students organize information/data using recommended structures. Manage self-determined processes (including teams) with multiple possible pathways.	Students organize information/data using self-determined structures and manage the processes (including team function) within the parameters set.	Students organize information/data using self-determined structures and management of processes (including team function).

(Continued)

Students' Autonomy When Researching

		Prescribed Researching	Bounded Researching	Scaffolded Researching	Open-ended Researching	Unbounded Researching
Analyze and synthesize *What does it mean?* Students analyze information/data critically and synthesize new knowledge to produce coherent individual/team understandings.	Creative	Students interpret given information/data and synthesize knowledge into prescribed formats. Sees patterns. *Ask emergent questions of clarification/curiosity*. Students communicate with each other and relate their understanding throughout set task. Use prescribed genre to develop and demonstrate understanding to a prescribed audience. Apply to a similar context the knowledge developed. Follow prompts on ECST issues.	Students interpret several sources of information/data and synthesize to integrate knowledge into standard formats. *Ask emergent, relevant, and researchable questions*.	Students analyze trends in information/data and synthesize to fully integrate component parts in structures appropriate to task. *Ask rigorous, researchable questions based on new understandings*.	Students analyses information/data and synthesizes to fully integrate component, consistent with parameters set. Fill knowledge gaps that are stated by others.	Students analyze and synthesize information/data to generalize or abstract knowledge that addresses self- or group-identified gaps in understanding.

Communicate and apply	Constructive					
How will we relate? Students discuss, listen, write, respond to feedback and perform the processes, understandings, and applications of the research, heeding ECST issues and needs of audiences.		Students communicate with each other and relate their understanding throughout set task. Use prescribed genre to develop and demonstrate understanding to a prescribed audience. Apply to a similar context the knowledge developed. Follow prompts on ECST issues.	Students use prescribed genre to develop and demonstrate understanding to a prespecified audience. Apply the knowledge developed to a similar context and follow prompts on ECST issues.	Students use some discipline-specific language and prescribed genre to demonstrate understanding from a stated perspective and for a specified audience. Apply to several similar contexts the knowledge developed and specify ECST issues.	Students use discipline-specific language and genres to demonstrate scholarly understanding for a specified audience. They apply the knowledge developed to diverse contexts and specify ECST issues in initiating, conducting, and communicating.	Students use appropriate language and genre to extend the knowledge of a range of audiences. Apply innovatively the knowledge developed to multiple contexts. Probe and specify ECST issues that emerge broadly.

What characterizes the move from "search" to "research"? Gathering more information and generating more data is merely a 'biggasearch'! Research is when students engage in all the above facets, time and again.

Research Skill Development (RSD), a conceptual framework for primary school to PhD, developed by John Willison and Kerry O'Regan, with much trialing by Eleanor Peirce and Mario Ricci. October 2006, revised March 2016. Facets based on Australian and New Zealand Institute for Information and Literacy (ANZIIL; 2004), Standards and Bloom's (1956) taxonomy. Extent of synthesis informed by the Structure of the Observed Learning Outcome (SOLO) taxonomy (Biggs & Collis, 1982). Note that framing researchable questions often requires a high degree of guidance and modelling for students, resulting from their synthesis (Red, Orange, Yellow) then initiating their research (Green and Blue). The six facets are often used directly with students as a 'learning routine' (Ritchhart & Perkins, 2008). The perpendicular font reflects dispositions towards research. Framework, resources, and references available at www.rsd.edu.au. Information: john.willison@adelaide.edu.au study. It provides a general progression from Facet A^2 through to Facet F (vertical axis):

- Embark/determine a need (issue/problem)
- Find/and generate (relevant information)
- Critically evaluate
- Organize
- Synthesize/analyze/apply
- Communicate (disseminate).

The learners' movement through the facets is recursive, as well as context-, task- and discipline-specific. The framework also provides the degree of autonomy (horizontal axis) or the extent that the learner requires structure and/or guidance to accomplish the task, thus, from the following:

- Prescribed Research: student research at the level of a closed inquiry (faculty-directed) and require a high degree of structure/guidance.
- Bounded Research: student research at the level of a closed inquiry and require some structure/guidance
- Scaffolded Research: student research independently at the level of a closed inquiry
- Open-ended Research: student research at the level of open inquiry (self-directed) within structured guidelines
- Unbounded Research/Open Inquiry (Student-directed): student research at the level of an open inquiry within self-determined guidelines in accordance with the discipline.

The framework helps students in teacher education programs to focus on the skill (facet) progression and on the dimension of learner autonomy while reinforcing their authentic self-directed learning. In addition, this framework provides common ground for communication in faculty-student scholarly collaboration. In sum, the RSD Framework

a   makes explicit and coherent the incremental attainment of research skills in any discipline or field of study.
b   provides a structure or framework for student progress across the skill developmental process.
c   serves as a platform for creating other models for the development of portable problem-solving skills in all areas of life (Willison, 2006–2018).

---

2   Each facet represents one aspect of the research process; the six facets are (i) embark/determine a need, (ii) find and generate, (iii) critically evaluate, (iv) organize, (v) synthesize/analyze/apply, and (vi) communicate.

Since this framework is easy to read, it is recommended as a tool that students can use to track their own learning through research, for example, analyze class assignments, evaluate out-of-class writing, or identify the parts of a journal article. Its overall benefits include improving students' self-directed learning (Brew & Saunders, 2020) and their participation in the change process regarding research in their teacher education programs.

Summary, Conclusion, and Implications

Overall, colleges and universities are invested in the promise of undergraduate research for all students; they frame strategic plans to support teaching and learning along with upgrades for infrastructure, extracurricular opportunities, and services to build and enrich the minds of the future (Gardner, 2006). Although the adoption of undergraduate research in professional schools, like schools of education, has proceeded at a pace slower than that in other disciplines, teacher educators to date have pursued creative and innovative ways to accelerate its pace through course-integrated research experiences.

This chapter set out first to initiate an informative and reflective journey with students in teacher education programs through the legacy of undergraduate research as enshrined in the benchmark Boyer Commission (1998) Report on undergraduate education. That report served as the starting point of the promise of transformation of higher education institutions. The chapter draws attention to students' responsibilities and the benefits that accrue from this inheritance. Finally, students are introduced to Willison and O'Regan's (2006) RSD framework as a tool for their self-directed learning. Overall, this chapter urges students in teacher education programs to (a) locate themselves in the history of higher education that shapes their undergraduate education, (b) knowingly claim that legacy of learning through research, and (c) assume the associated responsibilities of a persistent commitment to their own leaning and to their proposed professional choice.

Furthermore, this chapter sets the stage for students' engagement in the subsequent chapters, the layout of which has been systematically grouped to support both academic proficiencies and research-related dispositions. Chapter 2 introduces the research question as the central element of the research process. Chapter 3 focuses on the research literature with the promise that undergraduate researchers benefit from identifying, locating, and synthesizing the rich literature in educational research. These are followed by Chapter 4, "The Demands of Reading, Writing, and Thinking Like Researchers" and Chapter 5, "Technology: The All-Purpose Research Tool for Discovery, Organization, and Collaboration." These chapters support two key initial tasks: one related to the core competencies of reading, writing, and thinking (like a researcher) and the other on technological tools of research.

The text then introduces the next steps in the research process. Chapter 6 explains the tasks of building essential components of a research project: determining topic, research design, and ethical conduct need. Chapter 7 follows, addressing the *analysis of data, plus process methods and techniques*. Then comes Chapter 8, "Building Your Research Community with Peers, Near-peers, and Mentors," to remind students of the collaborative work that is a benchmark of the research environment. Subsequently, Chapters 9 and 10 together serve to guide the report-writing process. Chapter 9 helps student researchers to understand the results of their data analysis and to discern and communicate their meaning. Chapter 10 focuses on a most important part of the research process: disseminating the results and findings to multiple communities and on projecting next steps and future action related to your topic of interest.

Chapter 11 urges students to take research-related learning beyond the classroom and, in the process, to activate the practice of self-directed learning and to nurture learner autonomy and agency. For students in teacher education programs, the goal is about maximizing learner potential related to the application of research-related capacities.

The chapter layout and the text overall are designed with the students in mind: The hope is that first, with each step of the research process, the benefits from access to a range of capabilities (e.g., learning through research, contributing knowledge to the professional field, building toolkits of transferable skills, and developing self-advocacy) become evident, and, second, that the outcomes of becoming avid and engaged learners and professional agents are achieved: bearers of the rich legacy of (teacher) education, institutions' promise, and torchbearers and models to future generations of students in K-12 education.

References

Arneback, E., & Blåsjö, M. (2017). Doing interdisciplinarity in teacher education: Resources for learning through writing in two educational programs. *Education Inquiry*, 8(4), 299–312.Bandaranaike, S. (2018). From research skill development to work skill development. *Journal of University Teaching & Learning Practice*, 15(4). Article 7.

Bernini, M., & Woods, A. (2014). Interdisciplinarity as cognitive integration: Auditory verbal hallucinations as a case study. *Wiley Interdisciplinary Reviews: Cognitive Science*, 5(5), 603–612. Retrieved 2 3, 2021, from http://onlinelibrary.wiley.com/doi/10.1002/wcs.1305/abstract

Bloom, B. S. (1956). *Taxonomy of Educational Objectives, Handbook I: The Cognitive Domain*. New York: David McKay Co Inc.

Boyer Commission on Educating Undergraduates (1998). *Reinventing Undergraduate Education: A Blueprint for American Research Universities*. Stony Brook, NY: State University of New York. http://files.eric.ed.gov/fulltext/ED424840.pdf

Breen, R., Brew, A., Jenkins, A., & Lindsay, R.(2003). Designing the curriculum to link teaching and research. In *Reshaping Teaching in Higher Education*, Eds. A. Jenkins, R. Breen., R. Lindsay, & A. Brew (55–78). London: Routledge.

Brew, A., & Saunders, C. (2020). Making sense of research-based learning in teacher education. *Teaching and Teacher Education*, 87, 1–30.

Bundy, A. L., & Council of Australian University Librarians & Australian and New Zealand Institute for Information Literacy (ANZIIL) (2004). *Australian and New Zealand Information Literacy Framework: Principles, Standards and Practice.* Adelaide: Australian and New Zealand Institute for Information Literacy.

Crawford, L., & Shanahan, J. O. (2014). Undergraduate research in the fine arts at the college of Wooster. In *Creative Inquiry in the Arts and Humanities: Models of Undergraduate Research*, Eds. N. Y. Klos, J. O. Shanahan, & G. Young. Washington, DC: Council on Undergraduate Research, 23–32.

Crowe, J., & Boe, A. (2019). Integrating undergraduate research into social science curriculum: Benefits and challenges of two models. *Education Sciences*, 9. doi:10.3390/ educsci9040296

Gardner, H. (2006). *Five Minds for the Future: Cultivating Thinking Skills.*Cambridge, MA: Harvard Business School Press.

Hensel, N. H. (2018). *Course-Based Undergraduate Research: Educational Equity and High-Impact Practice Illustrated Edition.* Sterling, VA: Stylus Publishing.

Jabareen, J. (2009). Building a conceptual framework: Philosophy, definitions, and procedure. *Journal of Qualitative Methods*, 8(4), 49–62.

Kuh, G. D. (2008). *High-Impact Educational Practices: What They Are, Who Has Access to Them, and Why They Matter.* Washington, DC: Association of American Colleges and Universities.

Lopatto, D. (2007). Undergraduate research experiences support science career decisions and active learning. *CBE Life Science Education*, 6(4), 297–306. doi:10.1187/cbe.07-06-0039

Małachowski, M. (2019). Reflections on the evolution of undergraduate research at Primarily Undergraduate Institutions over the past 25 years. *Scholarship and Practice of Undergraduate Research*, 3(2), 38–45.

Manak, J. A., & Young, G. (2014). Incorporating undergraduate research into teacher education: Preparing thoughtful teachers through inquiry-based learning. *CUR: Quarterly*, 35(2), 35–38.

Mason, M. (2008) Complexity theory and the philosophy of education. *Education Philosophy and Theory,* 40(1), 4–18.

Miller, S. (2020). On the sum of k-th powers in terms of earlier sums (with Enrique Trevino), to appear in the College. *Mathematics Journal*, 48(2), 123–128.

Nishino, T. (2012). Multi-membership in communities of practice: An EFL teacher's professional development. *TESL-EJ* (Berkeley, Calif.), 16(2), 21–25.

Nolan, J. R., McConville, K. S., Addona, V., et al. (2020). Mentoring undergraduate research in statistics: Reaping the benefits and overcoming the barriers. *Journal of Statistics Education*, 28, 140–114.

Oliveira Medeiros, E. O. (2015). Education as interdisciplinary knowledge: Production, theory, and practice – in search of an essay. *European Scientific Journal*, August, 575–594.

Palmer, R. (2015). Establishing research apprenticeship options for prospective secondary teachers: A course-embedded model. *Scholar-Practitioner Quarterly (S-PQ)*, 9(1), 27–45.

Palmer, R. J., Hunt, A. N., Neal, M., & Wuetherick, B. (2015). Mentoring, undergraduate research, and identity development: A conceptual review and research agenda. *Mentoring and Tutoring*, 23(5), 1–16.

Puri, I. (2017). Unpublished Thesis: "On the Probability of Receiving a Top Choice Match." Awarded The Firestone Medal for Excellence in Undergraduate Research.

Ritchhart, R., & Perkins, D. N. (2008). Making thinking visible. *Educational Leadership*, 65(5), 57–61.

Rogoff, B. (2003). *The Cultural Nature of Human Development.* London: Oxford University Press.

Showman, A., Cat, L. A., Cook, J., Holloway, N., & Wittman, T. (2013). Five essential skills for every undergraduate researcher. *CUR Quarterly*, 13, 16–20.

Willison, J. W. (2018). Research skill development spanning higher education: Critiques, curricula and connections. *Journal of University Teaching & Learning Practice*, 15(4), 1–15.

Willison, J., & O'Regan, K. (2006). Research skill development framework. Retrieved from University of Adelaide: http://www.adelaide.edu.au/rsd/framework/rsd-framework.pdf.

2 Beginning the Investigation
The Research Question

Sylvia Tiala

Research Defined

We all ask questions. Who? What? When? Why? Where? How? We use these questions of inquiry every day (Sloan, 2010; Five Ws, 2021). Where can I find an apartment to rent? How do I make a favorite recipe? Why won't my car start? Our questions help us communicate, make inquiries, solve problems, and assess learning. But when do our questions become "research questions"? We need to define what we mean by "research" before we can investigate research questions.

What Is Research?

Research is discipline-specific inquiry (Fandino, 2019; OECD, 2015) with elements common across many contexts. For our purposes, we define research as a systematic, nonlinear, iterative, and ethical approach, linked to theory, that collects, analyzes, and interprets information from multiple sources to extend human knowledge beyond what is currently known (Biddix, 2018; Creswell, 2007, pp. 37–38; Leedy & Ormrod, 2015, p. 21; Mertler, 2016, p. 23; U.S. Department of Health & Human Services, n.d.; Willison & O'Regan, 2007). This definition incorporates multiple elements contributing to the overall definition of research. Table 2.1 below examines these elements and their contribution to the definition of research used within this chapter.

Begin with a Problem

According to Willison and O'Regan (2007), the research process begins with a sense of curiosity and observations in teaching and learning environments. This sense of curiosity helps individuals identify *research problems*. Research problems are found in issues or situations that others would be interested in knowing more about, such as areas of concern, conditions that could be improved, difficulties that need to be eliminated, and/or questions seeking answers (Association of College and Research Libraries [ACRL], 2019; Biddix, 2009).

DOI: 10.4324/9781003226475-2

Table 2.1 Elements of Educational Research

Systematic	The scientific method and its variations provide sequenced steps that researchers use in the development of their research project. Using a systematic approach keeps the researcher organized and effectively communicates research methodology to readers, reviewers, and other stakeholders interested in the study.
Nonlinear and iterative	Research models and methods are generally represented as neat linear or circular diagrams but do not reflect the messiness of the actual execution of the research process. Researchers need to be aware that research projects require flexibility, an openness to new ideas, identification of information gaps, and a willingness to view research as an inquiry process (ACRL, 1996–2021).
Ethical	Expected standards of conduct related to research are dictated by law, by professional associations, and by institutions. Truthfully presenting research data and protecting human/animal rights is important (Resnik, 2020). Check course, institutional, and association policies to make sure you comply with research protocols and the expectations of review boards before beginning research projects (ACRL, 2019).
Methodological approach	Your approach to research starts with the assumptions you make and a consideration of the scope of your project. Your approach considers data to be collected, the number of participants needed, data collection and analysis techniques, resource constraints, and the like (Mertler, 2016, pp. 6 & 25). The three approaches to research, beyond the scope of this chapter, are qualitative research, quantitative research, and mixed-methods research (Creswell, 2014; Leedy & Ormrod, 2015; Mertler, 2016)
Linked to theory	Theories help explain, predict, or understand phenomena. They help define hypotheses and inform your research questions (Johnson & Christensen, 2017; USC Libraries—Theoretical Framework, 2021). Tying your research study to a theoretical framework strengthens your study by explicitly calling out assumptions of your study and helping you provide a rationale for your research approach (USC Libraries—Theoretical Framework, 2021).
Collecting information	Researchers strategically search, evaluate, and gather information from a variety of credible sources knowing that conducting research is an iterative process (ACRL, 1996–2021).
Analyzing and interpreting information	Researchers critically analyze and interpret their data to produce coherent understanding and new knowledge (Willison & O'Regan, 2007)
Extending human knowledge	Educational research contributes to knowledge by addressing gaps in knowledge, expanding knowledge, replicating knowledge, or looking at questions from others' viewpoints (Biddix, 2018).

Identifying a research problem starts an individual on a path that applies the scientific method to educational research contexts. Mertler (2016, pp. 4–5) compared the similarities between the scientific method and educational research in a table like the one shown in Table 2.2. Mertler's chart has been modified to align the scientific method with Leedy and Ormrod's (2015, p. 21) seven-step research cycle, since the Leedy-Ormrod cycle is used as a framework for this chapter's organization. The comparison between Leedy and Ormrod's seven-step research cycle and the scientific method is also shown in Table 2.2.

Preservice teachers and practicing educators are well positioned to identify research problems. Through reflection and observation, you may ask questions such as, Is my teaching effective? How could I have improved today's lesson? Educators identify areas of concern, observe conditions that could be improved, and know of difficulties that need to be eliminated. Curiosity about these types of questions leads to the identification of research problems.

A real-life example of a research problem is found in a game design course (GD 101) focusing on educational elements of digital game creation. Students were interested in playing digital games for entertainment while the objectives of the course focused on game play for learning.

Table 2.2 Scientific Method Aligned to Educational Research

Research is an iterative, cyclical process that does not occur in a linear fashion!

Scientific Method	Educational Research
1 Clarify the main question inherent in the problem	1 Begin with a problem—an unanswered question
	2 Researchers clearly and specifically state the goal of the research endeavor
	3 Divide the principal problem into more manageable subproblems when appropriate
2 State a hypothesis	4 Formulate research questions and/or hypotheses concerning the specific problem or topic
	5 Develop a specific plan for addressing the problem and subproblems
3 Collect, analyze, and interpret information related to the question, such that it will allow you to provide an answer to that question	6 Collect, organize, and analyze data related to the problem and subproblems
4 Form conclusions derived from the interpretations of your analyses	7 Interpret the meaning and draw conclusions related to the problems and subproblems
5 Use your conclusions to verify or reject your original hypothesis	

The course instructor learned about *Games for Change* (2021) and its efforts to engage learners in social issues through game play. One of the games, *What the Frack* (Chen, Dodge, Osiecki, & Hicks, 2013), tackled the hydraulic fracturing debate from three different viewpoints. The game dovetailed nicely with a debate (Gerasimo, 2012) around sand fracking mines that were operating less than three miles away from the students' classroom. In the instructor's mind, the game was a perfect example of how game play and learning connected with real-world issues. Students reacted differently. As the game was introduced, their first reaction was that the game was about a politely stated swear word or associated with the Battlestar Galactica science fiction series. Only a handful of students were aware of the term "fracking" and its association with sand mining. During game play, students focused on the simplicity of the graphics, the lack of action, and an inability to "win." This situation prompted an *action research* study where the course instructor investigated her own teaching methods and theories in order to critically reflect and improve teaching practices (Johnson & Christensen, 2017, p. 58). In the GD 101 example the instructor combined the use of pre- and post-tests, with student analysis of their own data, to reflect on the potential of games as an educational tool. A simple fracking knowledge test was given to students before playing the fracking game, after playing the fracking game, and a third time after a class discussion about sand fracking and its impacts. Students were asked to record their times playing the fracking game but not to exceed 10 minutes of play. Results from time playing the fracking game and the pre- and post-tests were anonymized and given back to the students for analysis. A discussion about why the gains were made and how both game play and reflection improved test results ended the lesson. Student reflections on game play used for educational purposes were collected, allowing the instructor to gauge the impact of the instructional strategy on student learning.

Reflection Time: Brainstorm a list of research problems in your current teaching and learning setting (ACRL, 2019; Biddix, 2009). Consider looking in local newspapers for relevant problems, take time to read research articles, interview educators in your community, attend education-related conferences, or speak with peers who are also interested in educational research (Leedy & Ormrod, 2015, pp. 47–49). Try keeping a professional journal or create diary entries of topics that resonate with you (Arhar, Holly, & Kasten, 2001) if you are having trouble finding problems. Brainstorm as many ideas as possible using the following prompts:

• What questions do you have as you observe in classrooms, prepare to teach, or teach in a classroom or online environment?
• Are students learning? How do you know?

Figure 2.1 Clarifying the problem.

- What concerns do you have?
- What conditions need improvement?
- What education-related difficulties are you observing?

Articulating Research Problems and Identifying Subproblems

Much of the work in conducting educational research is clearly articulating a research problem and identifying the associated subproblems (Leedy & Ormrod, 2015). Clarifying your research goals takes the form of a problem statement that introduces readers to the importance of the topic you are studying and places your topic into a particular context (Biddix, 2018, pp. 30–31; USC Libraries—Research Problem, 2021). The rest of your study, including your research question, theoretical frameworks, and your research approach, will tie back to your problem statement (Mertler, 2016; USC Libraries—Research Problem, 2021). Identifying your problem statement can be visualized as shooting at a target with the intention of hitting the bullseye. The problem statement is the target that draws your attention away from the larger environment and creates a focus on one single problem to study.

Through **strategic exploration** (literature searches, interviews, observation, etc.) you identify others who have produced information about a topic (ACRL, 1996–2021). This preliminary literature search helps clarify your research problem, helps clarify subproblems, and provides methodological examples related to your topic. Visualize this initial exploration as target practice. In the beginning, you can hit the outer rings of the target. With more information from your "strategic explorations," you gain clarity on your research problem until you are able to "hit the bullseye" with targeted and viable research question(s).

Research Problem

We can walk through the process of creating a problem statement using the GD 101 example. A "research target" is created as the research problem is identified. Stating your research interest compares to drawing the outer-most ring of your target. At this point in the research process, your research problem is broadly stated. In the case of GD 101, that might be "This researcher is interested in investigating the impact of game play on students' learning."

Identifying Subproblems

Revisit your problem statement to look for subproblems that help lead toward your research questions. Leedy and Ormrod (2015, pp. 55–57) suggest mind mapping or using a paper-and-pencil technique. You will typically be able to identify two to six subproblems. If you identify many subproblems, you should revisit your problem statement to see whether it is more complex than you originally thought or whether your subproblems could be combined into larger subproblems (Leedy & Ormrod, 2015, p. 55). Two problems are indicated in the GD 101 example. First, students focus on elements of game play and not on the learning attributes of the game. Second, students are unaware of issues surrounding hydraulic fracking and its connections with health, environmental, and economic issues. The instructor did a brief search and found that students were more likely to get news from their phones while the instructor was getting news from television and newspapers (Kalogeropoulos, 2019).

A complete research problem statement indicating what was known, what was not known, and the importance of the research was created using the GD 101 example and Biddix's structure for describing research problems:

The first attempt at using an educational game to demonstrate learning gains to students enrolled in the GD 101 course was not successful. Students lacked the background knowledge enabling them to be able to identify educational elements of game play. The idea of playing an online digital game that addresses current events in the students' community should engage them as learners. However, students' news sources do not include local and area news. In addition, students have a broad range of experience associated with the topic of fracking. Some are aware of fracking and its related issues, while others have not heard of fracking outside of a science fiction context.

This researcher does not know where students are sourcing their news or their levels of interest with social issues and current events. It is uncertain whether game play can be used to simultaneously teach content (what is fracking and its impacts) and a conceptual understanding of learning (cognitive gains and affective gains). Another uncertainty is whether learning occurs because of game play or whether it is related to the students' processing of the game-playing experience.

Researching this topic is important for several reasons. Knowing whether game play can be used to simultaneously teach content and conceptual understandings will inform a procedural model, a set of steps, that the instructor can use to improve instruction. If effective, the model can be shared with other instructors as an effective teaching methodology. Using game play to construct a common experience among students may create more engaging lessons that increase student learning. Determining whether learning results from game play or the processing of game play will inform the current scholarly discussion related to the effectiveness of game play in learning environments.

Reflection Time: Create a problem statement. Review your list of brainstormed research problems and select three to five that most interest you. Write a short problem statement (1–2 paragraphs) for each of your problems using Biddix's (2018) structure. Your problem statements should achieve the following goals:

- Identify the problem. What is it that you are interested in researching?
- Describe what is known about the problem. Your preliminary strategic explorations will help you determine what is already known.
- Identify what is not known. Thinking about missing information will help you identify information gaps that may lead you to additional research questions.
- Explain why it is important to know what is not known. This will help you develop an argument justifying the importance of you work.

You may need to do additional investigative work and strategic exploring as you create your problem statements. Your explorations do not need to be exhaustive but do need to give you a sense of available resources that can support your research endeavors.

As you write your problem statements avoid using the word "prove" (Biddix, 2009; Leedy & Ormrod, 2015, p. 57). Remember that you are dealing with human beings who act and react differently based on internal (growth, physical health, mental health, etc.) and external (other people, technology, etc.) stimuli (Mertler, 2016, p. 9). Results from your study may not translate in the same way to individuals in a different time or place. Johnson and Christensen (2017, pp. 20–21) make a case for eliminating "prove" from research vocabulary and suggest that research is about finding "evidence" to support claims.

Up to this point you have been working with multiple research problems and problem statements. This is intentional. Not all research problems can be translated into feasible research projects, and some are more easily adapted than others. Remember the target analogy? Your continued efforts will move you closer and closer to the bullseye of your target. Let us work to narrow your research purpose statements to one that you will focus on. We will use criteria from Mertler (2016, pp. 8 & 9), Biddix (2009), Leedy and Ormrod (2015), and Notre Dame (n.d.), to evaluate your purpose statements. Take time to consider whether your research purpose statements

- have predetermined outcomes? If you answer "yes" to this question you should reframe or rethink the research purpose. Educational research does not have predetermined outcomes. Your options are to revise your research purpose or remove this item from further consideration as a viable research topic.
- have trivial outcomes? If you answer "yes" to this question you should remove this research problem from your list of viable topics.
- improve educational practice?
- improve the human condition?
- are researchable, given the resources available to you?
- are relevant to your field of study and/or to society at large?

Reflection Time: Evaluate your research problem statements for viability. Consider using a decision matrix, such as the one below, to help you choose between research problems. List your different research problems in the left-most vertical column. Then rate each of your problem statements with a score from 0 to 3 as indicated in the horizontal table header. Total the scores for each horizontal row to determine which research problem scores the highest. Choose the project you are most passionate about if there is a tied score.

	Predetermined Outcomes? 0 = Yes 1 = No	Trivial Outcomes 0 = Yes 1 = No	Ethically Conducted 0 = yes 1 = no	Improve Educational Practice 0 = No 1 = Little 2 = Moderate 3 = Much	Improve human condition 0 = No 1 = Little 2 = Moderate 3 = Much	Relevant to Your Field of Study/Society 0 = No 1 = Little 2 = Moderate 3 = Much	Total Score
Problem 1							
Problem 2							
Problem 3							
Problem 4							
Problem 5							

Remember that research is an iterative process. It is acceptable, even expected, that you may need to revise and rewrite your problem statements as more information and insights become available. Complete a secondary assessment of your research problem after you make any desired revisions. As suggested by Leedy and Ormrod (2015, pp. 53–54) ask yourself:

- Is the problem stated clearly and completely using grammatically correct sentences?
- Is your study focused?
- Is it clear you have an open mind about your end-results?
- Is it clear that you are inquiring and seeking evidence?
- Can you accomplish your project with the time, money, and effort available to you?
- Is this a problem you really want to investigate?

Get feedback from colleagues, peers, and instructors (if applicable) using the stated criteria and questions. Use their feedback to continue the revision process of your problem statement.

Theoretical Frameworks and Hypotheses/Questions

Research projects are tied to theoretical frameworks. The frameworks help readers understand the researcher's thinking process and help the researcher structure and justify a case for the research project. These theoretical frameworks, whether implied or overtly stated, impact your "philosophical worldview" (Creswell, 2014, pp. 5–19), your methodological approach, the hypotheses you choose, and ultimately the research questions you design.

Theoretical Framework

The GD 101 example used in this chapter is tied to theoretical frameworks and past research. Identifying these ties strengthens the teacher/researcher's justification for a research project. The GD 101 research problem uses an action research model that focuses on solving a particular problem by a practicing educator with the intention of improving teaching practices (Johnson & Christensen, 2017). It has its theoretical underpinnings in Kurt Lewin's force field and change theories as well as John Dewey's five phases of inquiry (Johnson & Christensen, 2017, pp. 59–62). In addition to the theoretical frameworks, games for educational purposes have been studied for several decades with a need for more research indicated (Ke, 2016). The idea of using a digital game to create a common experience for university students is informed by constructivist and adult learning theories (Huang, 2002).

Connecting research to theory takes time and effort. You will likely need to expand your knowledge about theories and frameworks through strategic exploration and literature review. Expect to move between literature review types of tasks and writing-related tasks as you move back and forth between the information you have and the information you need (ACRL, 1996–2021, Searching as strategic exploration). Research is an iterative process that depends on asking new and/or more complex questions (ACRL, 1996–2021—Research as inquiry). Think of the research process as a conversation you are having with other experts through a research process that occurs over an extended period (ACRL, 1996–2021—Scholarship is a conversation).

Reflection Time: Find two published studies in a scholarly journal that is related to your research problem. Be sure to reach out to a librarian if you need help with this task. As you read the articles, take time to write a one-page reflection for each study that addresses

- what problem is being studied?
- what theories and frameworks were referenced?
- who were the participants?
- where was the study conducted?
- how much time was needed to conduct the study?
- what types of questions are being asked (e.g., How, What, Why, Does)?
- what variables are identified in the study?
- how were data collected (interviews, surveys, observation, etc.)?
- what methodological approaches were used in the study (qualitative, quantitative, mixed methods)?
- what other observations you make to inform your own study?

Hypotheses/Questions

It is time to start constructing the inner rings of the research target you are building. By now you should be generating your own ideas about the systems, processes, and other factors associated with your research problem. You can apply concepts from your readings and use your experience to predict (create hypotheses) what may be learned from your study (Creswell, 2014, p. 139). Do you have hunches about what you think you might learn as the result of conducting a study related to your research problem?

The GD 101 example uses both hypotheses (Leedy & Ormrod, 2015, p. 57) and general questions. Hypotheses are generated before the study begins (a priori) and stated in a way that avoids certainty. Remember that at the end of a research study the hypotheses may not be supported by the evidence. Hypotheses used to inform the quantitative aspects of the GD 101 action research may include the following:

- There may be a relationship between the time learners spend playing an educational game and how much they learn.
- There may be a relationship between post game-play group discussions and how much students learn.

Qualitative aspects of the GD 101 action research focused on adult learning principles applied to traditionally aged university students. The instructor refrained from speculating about findings and (Leedy & Ormrod, 2015, p. 58) wondered

- how does increasing students' awareness of social issues, such as fracking, influence the likelihood of their engaging with the issue?
- what teaching practices help game design students understand the elements of game play that impact learners' cognitive and affective learning?

Reflection Time: Create a list of hypotheses and questions that you could develop into final research questions. Be sure that your hypotheses and questions remain aligned to your research statement. Remember that research is an iterative process so updating and revising your research problem and theoretical frameworks is acceptable.

Research Purpose and Research Questions

It is time to start focusing on the inner rings of your research target. In this section, we bring all your hard work together in a finalized draft of your research purpose and the associated research question(s). Think about the purpose of your research and what you want to accomplish. Will you be doing a quantitative study that tries to explain or predict phenomena, test a theory, or communicate results using statistics or numbers? Will you be describing, explaining, interpreting phenomena, or building theory and communicating results through narratives, quotations, or using personal voice in a qualitative study? Leedy and Ormrod (2015, p. 99) summarize the characteristics of qualitative and quantitative research methods in ways that help connect methodology to research purpose.

Research Purpose

Generating research questions begins by restating the research problem using a research purpose statement that includes specifics (Mertler, 2016, pp. 40–41). The need for specificity requires a researcher to identify who the study participants will be, what research methodologies will be used, where the study will take place, and the like. Mertler (p. 41) suggests that researchers should work to identify the variables ("characteristics that differs from one individual, object, procedure or setting") and the constants ("traits that do not differ") when creating their purpose statement. Leedy and Ormrod (2015, pp. 58–61) explain and illustrate independent and dependent variables that in a way that researchers may find useful. Revisiting the Five Ws + How (Five Ws, 2021) also helps researchers think about the level of detail needed to create a research purpose statement:

- Who will I be studying? Be specific with demographics such as age, gender, ethnicity, and the like.
- What variables will be used in forming research questions?
- How will I conduct the study? Identify what methodology you will use to recruit participants and collect data.
- What resources will I need to conduct my study? Consider the constraints that challenge your work not limited to time, materials, funding, partnerships, and the like.
- Where will the study occur? Will you be working at a site that is easily accessible or will you need to travel to other locations?
- When will the study occur? Determine a timeline for implementation of your research.
- Why is this study important? This should already be addressed if you have created a problem statement.

The GD 101 example uses a mixed-method format and has both quantitative and qualitative elements in the purpose statement.

> This mixed method study, conducted with sophomore to senior level students enrolled in XYZ University's GD 101 course, will investigate the impact of game play on students' learning using quantitative and qualitative data collected in parallel, analyzed separately, and then merged. The quantitative portion of the study uses time spent playing an educational game and discussion participation as the independent variables. Students' abilities to define fracking and identify impacts of fracking on a written assessment are the independent variables. Themes from students' responses to open ended questions about their learning will help the instructor determine if game play, students' analysis of data, and discussions are effective methods in helping game design students understand how educational games impact learning. The reason for collecting both quantitative and qualitative data is to gain a more holistic picture of student learning.

Reflection Time: Create a purpose statement for your problem statement. Generate a more specific problem statement using the format like the GD 101 example. Remember that this example serves as a general guide, and you should adapt your writing to your context. Consider whether you will use a qualitative or quantitative approach as you generate your research purpose statements. Leedy and Ormrod (2015, pp. 97–102) summarize the different approaches in their online text. Creswell (2014, pp. 126–134) provides generic scripts for drafting qualitative, quantitative, and mixed-methods purpose statements.

Research Questions

What is a research question? In simple terms, a research question is a question that addresses your research problems and purpose. You have just completed the process that identifies these problems and purposes. It is time to complete your target by creating the "bullseye," that is, your research question(s). Your research questions are important as they will guide the rest of your research processes, the study that you conduct, and the research results you communicate to others. For example, the quantitative research questions associated with the GD 101 example are:

Research Question 1: Does the amount of time students play *What the Frack* impact their ability to define fracking on a teacher-generated test?
Research Question 2: Does the amount of time students play *What the Frack* impact their ability to identify impacts of fracking on a teacher-generated test?

The qualitative elements of the games in education mixed-method study could be addressed by interviewing students and asking questions such as follows:

1 Please describe what you learned as the result of playing *What the Frack* and participating in the classroom discussions.
2 What are your perceptions of using games to teach content in an educational setting?
   a What or who influenced these beliefs (as a follow-up question if appropriate)?

Johnson and Christensen (2017) provide scripts for writing quantitative research questions that reflect a descriptive, predictive, or causal research approach. Descriptive questions answer "How" or "What" questions and are used to describe variables and/or relationships between variables. Predictive questions are structured so that a predictor variable predicts an outcome variable in a particular setting. Causal questions are structured to compare how a change in an independent variable produces change in dependent variables (p. 97).

Creswell (2014) provides a structure for generating qualitative research questions indicating that the research questions start with "What" or "How" statements. The idea that qualitative research questions focus on a single concept that develops over time is conveyed using exploratory verbs indicating that the research will report, reflect, describe, discover, explore, seek to understand, and the like (pp. 139–141). The researcher's expectation for the qualitative research question to evolve or change over time is reflected in Creswell's typical script for one (2014, p. 141).

Guidelines for writing research questions, such as the ACRL's (2019), provide a helpful reference when constructing research questions. Clearly stated questions demonstrate a researcher's clarity of thinking and helps readers follow along in the research process. One should be mindful of the resources that are available and structure their research project, and the related research questions, accordingly. Investigations should be focused and feasible given the constraints of the project. The significance of research questions should be considered. Are there other individuals, besides the researcher, who might learn something from the work? Finally, questions should be structured in a way that facilitates the fair and ethical treatment of human beings and/or animals that are involved in a study. Institutional policies and review boards are in place to help protect study participants from harm. Proper protocols and procedures should be followed as the research project moves forward (ACRL, 2019; Notre Dame, n.d.).

Reflection Time: Write your research questions using the ACRL (2019) and Notre Dame (n.d.) guidelines. As you write, ask yourself:

- Are my research questions stated clearly?
- Do I have the necessary time, budget, and other resources to answer these questions?
- Do my questions appropriately focus on the research problem and purpose?
- Are there others who might learn something from the research questions I am asking?
- Can my research be conducted ethically?

Use the listed bullet points as you request feedback from colleagues, peers, and instructors (if applicable). Use their feedback to revise your research questions.

Importance of Research Questions

Why are research questions important? Throughout this chapter the importance of research questions has been addressed by focusing on the creation of a viable research project and its associated research questions. Biddix (2009) sums up the importance of a research question as follows: "A research question is the fundamental core of a research project, study, or review of literature. It focuses the study, determines methodology, and guides all stages of inquiry, analysis, and reporting." But research questions are important for additional reasons.

Research questions succinctly capture the essence of a research project. This becomes important as researchers communicate their ideas to others. Researchers may need collaborators to complete a research project. Clearly stated research questions help recruit these additional collaborators. Many researchers need additional funds to conduct their research. The research question serves as a succinct way to convey the research purposes to potential funders. Conveying results after a research project has been completed is an expectation of research endeavors. The research question helps frame study results as the conclusions and implications are released to broader audiences. In this case, the research question becomes a foundational piece of informational and marketing campaigns.

Implicit in your ability to generate research questions is the fact that you have developed the knowledge and practices inherent in information literacy skills (ACRL, 1996–2021) and research processes (Willison & O'Regan, 2007). The ability to generate and act upon research questions provides evidence to school administrators, employers, and departments of education that you possess problem-solving, reflection, and employability skills necessary to be successful in job settings. Your ability to generate and act upon research questions signals to school officials your commitment to being a reflective practitioner who is committed to creating the best learning environment possible.

Take time to complete one final reflection before moving on to the next chapter. How does generating research problems and research skills apply to you and your context? What value does the ability to generate research questions add to your professional, and perhaps personal, life?

References

ACRL (1996–2021). *Framework for information literacy for higher education.* http://www.ala.org/acrl/standards/ilframework.

ACRL (2019). *College & research libraries guide for authors & reviewers.* https://acrl.libguides.com/c.php?g=525633&p=3593255

Arhar, J. M., Holly, M. L. & Kasten, W. C. (2001). *Action research for teachers: Traveling the yellow brick road.* Upper Saddle River, NJ: Prentice-Hall, Inc.

Biddix, J. P. (2009). *What is educational research?* https://researchrundowns.com/intro/whatisedresearch/

Biddix, J. P. (2018). *Research methods and applications for student affairs.* San Francisco, CA: John Wiley & Sons.

Chen, H., Dodge, B., Osiecki, K. & Hicks, A. (2013, January 27) *What the frack.* https://www.gamesforchange.org/game/what-the-frack/

Creswell, J. W. (2007). *Qualitative inquiry & research design: Choosing among five approaches* (2nd ed.). Thousand Oaks, CA: Sage. https://www.academia. edu/33813052/Second_Edition_QUALITATIVE_INQUIRY_and_ RESEARCH_DESIGN_Choosing_Among_Five_Approaches

Creswell, J. W. (2014). *Research design: Qualitative, quantitative, and mixed methods approach* (4th ed.). Thousand Oaks, CA: Sage.

Fandino, W. (2019, August). Formulating a good research question: Pearls and pitfalls. *Indian Journal of Anaesthesia 63*(8), 611–616. https://www.ncbi.nlm.nih. gov/pmc/articles/PMC6691636/

Five Ws. (2021, May 26). *Wikipedia.* https://en.wikipedia.org/wiki/Five_Ws

Games for Change. (2021). *Who we are.* https://www.gamesforchange.org/ who-we-are/

Gerasimo, P. (2012, April 27). *Mining companies invade Wisconsin for frac-sand.* https:// www.ecowatch.com/mining-companies-invade-wisconsin-for-frac-sand- 1881611705.html

Huang, H. (2002). Toward constructivism for adult learners in online learning environments. *British Journal of Educational Technology 33*(1), 27–37. https://bera- journals.onlinelibrary.wiley.com/doi/epdf/10.1111/1467-8535.00236

Johnson, R. B. & Christensen, L. (2017). *Educational research: Quantitative, qualitative, and mixed approaches* (6th ed.). Thousand Oaks, CA: Sage.

Kalogeropoulos, A. (2019). *How younger generations consume news differently.* https://www.digitalnewsreport.org/survey/2019/how-younger-generations- consume-news-differently/

Ke, F. (2016). Designing and integrating purposeful learning in game play: A systematic review. *Educational Technology Research Development 64*, 219–144. https://doi.org/10.1007/s11423-015-9418-1

Leedy, P. D. & Ormrod, J. E. (2015). *Practical research: Planning and design* (11th ed.). Essex: Pearson. https://pce-fet.com/common/library/books/51/2590_%5 BPaul_D._Leedy,_Jeanne_Ellis_Ormrod%5D_Practical_Res(b-ok.org).pdf

Mertler, C. (2016). *Introduction to educational research.* Thousand Oaks, CA: Sage Publications.

Notre Dame (n. d.). *Developing a research question.* https://library.ndnu.edu/ researchbasics/researchquestion.

OECD. (2015). *Frascati manual 2015: Guidelines for collecting and reporting data on research and experimental development. The measurement of scientific, technological and innovation activities.* Paris: OECD Publishing. doi: http://dx.doi. org/10.1787/9789264239012-en.

Resnik, D. B. (2020, December 23). *What is ethics in research & why is it important.* https://www.niehs.nih.gov/research/resources/bioethics/whatis/index.cfm

Sloan, M. (2010). Aristotle's Nicomachean ethics as the original locus for the septem circumstantiae. *Classical Philology 105*(3), 236–251. https://doi. org/10.1086/656196

U.S. Department of Health & Human Services. (n. d.). *Module 1: Introduction: What is research?* https://ori.hhs.gov/module-1-introduction-what-research.

USC Libraries-Research Problem. (2021, June 4). *Research problem.* https://lib- guides.usc.edu/writingguide/introduction/researchproblem

USC Libraries-Theoretical Framework. (2021, June 4). *Theoretical framework.* https://libguides.usc.edu/writingguide/theoreticalframework

Willison, J., & O'Regan, K. (2007). Commonly known, commonly no known, totally unknown: A framework for students becoming researchers. *Higher Education Research and Development 26*(4), 393–409.

3 Building a Foundation for Undergraduate Research in Teacher Education

The Literature Review

Suzanne F. Lindt and Emily N. Smith

At the center of any undergraduate research project, whether qualitative or quantitative,[1] is the review of the research literature (or "literature review"): the analysis and synthesis of the published academic research related to a specific topic. When you complete a literature review successfully, you can accrue many benefits, including confidently building a sure foundation for the research project, being assured about your capacity to identify and locate the relevant scholarly literature, and through concentrated study, understanding what is known and/or not known about a topic (Denney & Tewksbury, 2013). In addition, you will learn to think critically about what gaps or questions continue to exist in the field of study (Zorn & Campbell, 2006).

Further benefits include being able to establish parameters on the topic/s and justify the reason for conducting a study (Zorn & Campbell, 2006) by using thoroughly developed research questions for your own study (Denny & Tewksbury, 2013). However, beyond these academic literacy skills and competencies, completing the literature review successfully enhances self-confidence in pursuing an area of interest, persistence, and even risk-taking and vulnerability, especially when you share the products of the literature review with peers and mentors.

Chapter Overview

This chapter presents a detailed, step-by-step layout of how to write a high-quality literature review with special attention given to establishing the source and value of the resources (including print, non-print, photographic, and digital resources) used to build the literature review. The twin goals are first to present this task as a strategic learning process that ensures the practice and adoption of multiple transferable skills that have implications for immediate and continuing academic and professional maturity, and second, to provide student researchers with specific strategies to create a review of literature with an advisor or mentor or to create the review of literature as an independent endeavor.

DOI: 10.4324/9781003226475-3

The chapter is divided into five distinct yet interrelated sections. The first section addresses the researcher's readiness to learn in the face of a new and complex task; it also provides verified approaches to deconstruct challenging tasks and help to set the social and emotional dispositions that support continuing engagement. The second section focuses on identifying and locating essential research sources; it also identifies on-campus and electronic resources that are available to support research efforts. The third section lays out in systematic fashion the tasks and corresponding strategies that help in the organization, analysis, and synthesis of the identified academic sources. The role of self-assessment and feedback is addressed in Section 4, which emphasizes the use of course/task rubrics and the need for openness to peer and instructor critique of your work. Finally, the fifth section focuses on dissemination of the work as an essential part of the research process, and the work ends with a concise summary, conclusion, and recommendations to guide future research.

Step I. Readiness to Learn: Facing Complexity and Possibility

In the face of any new or perceived challenging task, learners, researchers included, need to pause long enough to consider and consciously determine their own learning readiness (i.e., how to establish strategic plans to seek out knowledge and participate in one's own learning in addition to understanding the task). Doing that includes a quick yet realistic scan of (a) one's ability to understand and to complete the task and (b) past experiences with learning, both positive and negative.

This section is focused on the preparatory information and dispositions needed to begin the tasks of the literature review: establishing a clear definition of the task, researcher's dispositions, and additional benefits of the literature review. Completing a high-quality literature

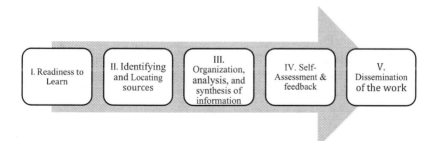

Figure 3.1 Steps to writing the review of literature.

review requires a researcher to first *identify and locate* the media and information sources, and then, to *analyze and synthesize* the sources, presenting the literature review in a coherent and compelling manner (Figure 3.1).

Most universities offer a variety of services available to help students begin their journey of writing the literature review. The following services and support may be available at your university:

- Libguides[2]/research guides
- Library information courses that are open to all students
- Reading/writing centers
- Media centers
- Office of Undergraduate Research
- Department advisors/mentors (office hours).

References to these and other available supports are threaded throughout this chapter; they serve to call attention to and prompt the practice of help-seeking behaviors that, along with other characteristics of learning readiness, enhance goal achievement.

Understanding the Task: What Is a (High-Quality) Review of the Literature?

Whatever the content or topic, the process of completing a high-quality literature review requires focused attention to and mastery of distinct yet interrelated skill sets, including (a) identify needed information, (b) locate them in academic databases, (c) organize/analyze the information, and (d) synthesize and/or use the information. These skill sets are embedded in Media and Information Literacy (MI&L).

Media literacy is the ability to identify different types of media and the messages they are sending. These include print media such as newspapers, magazines and posters, and theatrical presentations, as well as tweets, radio broadcasts, and communication outlets or tools used to store and deliver information or data.

Information literacy is the ability to articulate one's information needs and the ability to identify, locate, and access appropriate sources of information to meet the information need. It also includes effective use of information resources, regardless of format, and the ability to apply the information critically and ethically.

The literature review engages researchers in those activities (Learning by doing, Learning how to learn, Learning through inquiry)[3] that guarantee proficiency in M&IL (Figure 3.2).

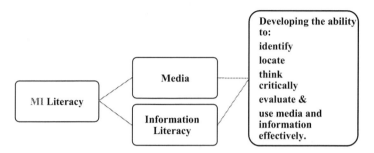

Figure 3.2 Elements of media and information literacy.

Step II. Identifying and Locating Sources

Whatever the topic/content or its originating source (a class assignment or an independent study), the procedures for gathering resources for the literature review are the same:

1 Identifying keywords and search terms
2 Understanding research databases
3 Searching the databases
4 Sorting materials
5 Finding available resources.

Identifying Keywords and Search Terms

A well-defined research topic guarantees an advantageous start for the literature review. It offers quick identification and recognition of the relevant subject, with clearly recognized areas of focus, and other guiding factors that provide the initial direction for the identification of keywords or search terms. The accuracy and relevance of these keywords/search terms are critical since they serve to launch the next step in the process—the database search.

The steps for identifying keywords and search terms:

1 Beginning with the title (or the research question), select the significant and relevant words/concept or phrases. These will serve as your initial *keywords* or *search words*.
2 For each word/concept, make a list of other words with the same or related meaning (synonyms).
3 Check appropriateness of search words by using the online thesaurus. The thesaurus may also help the researcher find more specific terms that are closer to the meaning intended; this helps to yield a more precise outcome (Table 3.1).

Table 3.1 Identifying Search Terms/Keywords

Research Topics	Initial Search Terms	Refine Using the Thesaurus
Understanding how **movement** in the classroom affects **student learning in early childhood**	– "movement" and "learning" – "movement" "in the classroom," and "student learning" – "Early childhood"	– Various types of movements – Learning? – Boys and/or girls
Explaining **high school students' reasoning** related to **ethical** and **moral issues**	– "High school student/adolescent" "moral beliefs" – "ethics" – "Adolescent moral beliefs" and "reasoning skills	– High school/secondary school

With keywords and search terms identified, you can continue to the next step—identification and location of the information using the databases.

Understanding Research Databases

Research databases facilitate information gathering in support of research and other information-gathering projects. They are organized collections of computerized information or data. These databases usually provide access to hundreds of different education-related journals that provide researchers with a variety of materials, including scholarly and peer-reviewed journal articles published by credible authors and experts in their field and magazine articles, books or encyclopedias, graphics/charts, images, charts, and primary sources and multimedia. Research databases can be general or subject-oriented, with bibliographic citations, abstracts, and/or full-text articles and can provide powerful search tools for narrowing results—users can more quickly find the information they need.

An appropriate activity at this point is to browse the library website of any institution; seek out education-specific and education-related databases (as explained below). Each library has its defined collection of databases, but libraries together ensure exchange of materials through their interlibrary loan system, with a quick turnaround for electronic or hardcopy materials.

Education-Specific Databases

A variety of databases are available, and many are specific to academic disciplines. Check with your advisor or mentor to ensure that you utilize the most appropriate database for the project. Some education-specific databases available to researchers include the following: Primary Search,

Middle Search, MAS Ultra School Education, Education Resources Information Center (ERIC), and Academic Search Premier (EbscoHost Search Platform).[4]

However, since education is an interdisciplinary field, education researchers may also benefit from using interdisciplinary databases (e.g., women and gender studies, world languages and cultures) and those dedicated to other relevant disciplines (e.g., PsychInfo).

Searching the Databases

With the search term/phrases and/or keywords, you should first attempt a simple search using the steps below and enter brief, general, keywords, and phrases.

1   Select the databases appropriate for your topic.
2   Make notes from each database to keep track of your search.
3   Start searching using subject headings, keywords, search words, or phrases. Start with simple searches, then move to more advanced searches.

After completing some simple searches, you will be ready to limit your search results to uncover more specific information. Complete the remaining steps for a more advanced search:

4   Using Boolean logic/operators.[5] Limit the search by year, recognizing benchmark documents outside of your limit.
5   Browse articles/materials to ensure that they can in fact contribute to your focus.
6   Begin the selection in terms of numbers of sources needed.
7   Request interlibrary loan if needed.
8   Seek help from the faculty-librarian.

Sorting Materials by Types and Other Classification

After gathering information from the databases, begin sorting the gathered information. There are several different ways to consider sorting sources, including primary versus secondary, classic versus benchmark studies, relevance of research studies, and provenance of the author.

Primary versus Secondary Sources

It is important to determine the type of source (primary or secondary), date of publication, and the author(s), with their affiliation (i.e., with which college, university, or other institution they are affiliated; Table 3.2).

Table 3.2 Definitions of Primary and Secondary Sources

Primary sources are original works conducted by a researcher on a specific topic; they represent original thinking, often include new findings and novel arguments. These are both quantitative and qualitative works. Primary sources also serve as models for beginning researchers.	*Secondary sources* summarize research from others in the field. These sources can be valuable to summarize previous research in the field and to suggest gaps in the literature. It is often recommended to beginning researchers to read secondary sources first, to get a panoramic view of the topic/s at hand.

Sources can be easily identified by first reading the abstracts carefully and then skimming articles/documents to confirm the relevance to your topic. It is generally recommended to use both types of sources: secondary sources to provide the state of research on the topic, and primary sources to draw attention to the investigation of specific researchers or research teams (Denny & Tewksbury, 2013).

Classic/Benchmark and Recent/Current Studies

A study/report gains a benchmark/classic designation when its work contributes to or significantly influences a field of study. For example, Piaget's Theory of Cognitive Development (1936) changed the way educators think about learning and thinking. Piaget explained a new theory that claimed that intelligence is based on the natural development and exploration of a child through four different life stages. Some of his assertions still influence educational practices today. Ames (1992) defined *achievement goal theory*, which explained the reasons (mastery or task) that learners establish goals for learning and achievement. Subsequent research studies on achievement goal theory have made suggestions for teaching and learning. If published within the previous ten years, studies are usually considered "recent" or "current." It is important to note that today, in the rapid flow of information, materials become obsolete in shorter periods of time. It is important to check for the most current information on any issue.

Relevance of Research Studies

Determining the relevance of research studies is critical to ensure that the resources you choose are closely related to your chosen topic. Though searches may reveal numerous results, students should make sure that the chosen studies are focused on similar content of the study and the nature of the argument being made. Review an article/document thoroughly using earlier recommendations to make a judgment about its relevance to the task at hand.

Provenance of the Author

Important also in the selection of studies is the background, credentials/ areas of expertise, prior and current work/publications, and institutional affiliation of the author(s). These factors contribute to the credibility of the source, which provide a stronger resource by which to justify the current study.

Finding Available Resources

To assist you with organizing and selecting information, resources may be available on campus or on the web.

Library and Faculty Librarians as Resource

Library searches—identifying and locating resources—can be challenging to researchers even when they may be following clear steps outlined for the task. However, library personnel/faculty support the academic life of their institutions and their communities and are available in person and online at many institutions. Thus, researchers can access the library supports through the faculty and discipline-specific librarian who have a central role in raising awareness, developing models, advocating for policy, and supporting their university in maintaining an infrastructure that supports research (Meulemans & Carr, 2012). Today, with online access to information, the roles of faculty librarians in undergraduate research are enhanced: Faculty librarians work collaboratively with teaching faculty to support students' library work. Undergraduate researchers must activate their help-seeking behaviors by using the protocols established by their instructors, mentors, and librarians themselves; they are valuable assets to the process of identifying, locating, and selecting sources.

Technology Tools

In addition to the tools and resources available to you at the library and on campus, students may also rely on additional sources, for example Google Scholar, which also has access to many articles and books related to various education topics.

Step III. Organizing, Analyzing, and Synthesizing Academic Sources

Whatever the topic/content or its originating source (a class assignment or an independent study), the procedures for **organizing, analyzing, and synthesizing** of the sources are the same. These procedures for each step are presented below.

Organize

Assemble, skim, scan, group using criteria (e.g., topic/s), read, and reread the sources in printed or electronic format. Begin with the abstract and the discussion section at the end of the source to identify specific parts of the article (e.g., purpose). Read the article in its totality using in-depth reading approaches.

The abstract usually provides a background on the research study, a summary of research methods used, and the findings. The discussion section is where the author examines the underlying meaning of the investigation, its implications, and the possible improvements that can be made to further develop the concerns of the work.

Reading is a complex activity: It takes time and requires focused attention and thought even when interest is only in scanning or skimming and/ or in-depth reading. It benefits the researcher to complete the following:

- Read actively—write in the margins, highlight phrases, take note of important points.
- Examine diagrams and figures, as they contain important information.
- Read critically—ask yourself questions about the text (e.g., what is the purpose of this work? Is the argument logical?)

When reading for understanding (in-depth reading), use approaches that support the effort, for example, making connections across content and the author's logic, predicting next steps, questioning or interrogating the text, monitoring self in the process to avoid distractions, visualizing, and summarizing to capture details of content.

To be successful in this task, researchers must practice patience with self and the task, and they should persist despite the challenge. Do not change the assignment. The good news here is that with practice, you will become more organized, efficient, and proficient.

Analyze

After organizing the information gathered, begin to analyze it. You can do this in various ways, but, most importantly, you need to find the way that works best for you and for your research. During the process, you should keep notes, for example, notecards, electronic folders, graphic organizers, or other data visuals for notetaking or prepare an annotated bibliography.

Graphic Organizers and Electronic Folders

A graphic organizer/SmartArt tool is a visual tool that allows researchers to make pictures of and organize the ideas; they show the relationships between concepts or themes in research.

Electronic folders serve a similar function; they provide a way to manage the sources by indicating levels, associations, and occurrences.

Annotated Bibliography

An annotated bibliography is a short summary and/or critical evaluation of each source, including its full citation. Researchers often use the annotated bibliography in their attempts to better understand the content of each source. See sample below.

Sample Annotated Bibliography

Lindt, S. F., & Rutherford, E. (2017). The impact of student achievement goals and engagement on students' writing improvement. *Special Education Research, Policy, & Practice, 1*(1), 63–75.

This study investigated the relationship between middle-school students' achievement goals and classroom engagement to their writing scores throughout a school year. Student writing samples were collected in the fall and spring of one school year to calculate student writing improvement. Students self-reported their academic achievement goals and class engagement in the spring. Results of hierarchical linear regression suggest that students' behavioral engagement positively predicted writing improvement, while emotional engagement and behavioral disengagement negatively predicted writing improvement. Findings suggest that writing teachers may need to increase strategies to keep students behaviorally engaged in the classroom in order to improve struggling writing over the school year.

Synthesize

Combine the different pieces of information into a coherent whole. This requires concisely summarizing and linking/integrating different sources to best present a reasoned and logical document, which, in this case, is a review of the literature.

Create an Outline

The earlier mapping of your sources, with some elaboration, is the basis of this outline—a general plan of what you are going to write in the finished paper. It shows the order of your information, what each section/paragraph will discuss, and so on. This outline represents a hierarchical way to display related items of text to graphically depict their relationships. Note that as you proceed, you may/will adjust the outline to enhance the quality and flow text.

Writing the Literature Review

Here the outline becomes important. While the literature review follows the basic essay format (Introduction, Body, Conclusion), and since here the literature itself is the topic of the essay, it is important to consider the literature in terms of its topics/themes as outlined. Snyder (2019) argues for five components to a literature review: (1) Abstract or a summary of the lit review (generally written at the end of the review); (2) Introduction with purpose and overview (how the work is laid out); (3) Main parts of the work are organized in sections to present and discuss the themes identified through the review of documents; (4) Summary, Conclusion, and Recommendations with implications for continuing work; and (5) Bibliography/References/Citations—a list of all the sources in required format.

Academic Writing

Make sure that academic writing is clear, concise, focused, structured, and supported by evidence. Its purpose is to explain some idea or research finding and specially to persuade readers that the explanations presented are plausible.

The four main types of academic writing appear in literature reviews: descriptive, analytical, persuasive, and critical. Each of these types of writing has its specific language features and purposes and conventions. However, it follows all the steps of the writing process—prewriting, drafting, revising, and editing.

Ethical Concerns

Paraphrasing information extracted from the sources constitutes the building blocks of good writing. It involves a restatement or rewording of a text or passage giving the meaning in a form different from the original work; as such, it is both a beginning and a reminder of the ethical use of sources. A citation at the end of the paraphrase signals that the words are the writer's, but the thought is from the author cited. The practice and the perfecting of paraphrasing helps the research avoid any semblance of plagiarism.

Format

Generally, education researchers use the format of the American Psychological Association (APA). The current manual is available online and in hardcopy. For a sample paper, written in APA format/style, visit the APA Style website (http://www.apastyle.org).

Campus Resources

There are many other departments on campus that provide writing assistance. Undergraduate researchers are advised to access and benefit from their support for the literature review.

Writing Centers. The services of campus writing centers/labs are available at no cost to student researchers. Their peer mentoring programs are at the center of their offerings. According to Ervin (2016, p. 47), in addition to writing help, peer mentors can assist with the organization/reorganization of sources, outline development, and editing.

Undergraduate Research Office or other campus resources. Additional help with resources and writing may be available at other campus offices, including the Office of Undergraduate Research. It is recommended that student researchers seek out and access all the resources that are available to them on campus and the many resources that exist beyond those in control of the faculty members and campus librarians.

Step IV. Self-Assessment and Feedback

When a first draft of a literature review has been completed, it is important to put a pause on the celebration—to complete two important tasks: a quality assurance self-check or a self-evaluation, and to solicit feedback from peers, advisors, or faculty instructor. The first is an integral part of self-directed learning; the second is an extension of help-seeking behaviors, yet together they reinforce the power of reflective practice and of learning as a social endeavor.

Rubrics

Rubrics are useful in the evaluation of the quality of your literature review. As scoring guides, they evaluate a performance, a product, or a project. It has three parts: (1) performance criteria, (2) rating scale, and (3) indicators. It defines what is expected and what will be assessed and serves to ensure that the review meets the expectation of the assignment. An assignment rubric is a useful self-evaluation tool. Using self-evaluation rubrics requires that researchers adopt an honest stance to benefit from their purpose—to enhance the quality of the work. Rubrics make the positives and negative qualities of the work transparent and thus available for improvement and enhancement.

Soliciting feedback from peers and others engages the researcher/learner in a process in which she or he makes sense of information about a performance or project and uses it to enhance the quality of the work. Seeking feedback is a part of the art of collaboration and consultation. While sometimes challenging, you should assume the role of an active participant in the process, be receptive to suggestions and recommendations.

Consulting with Peers

Peers bring unique perspectives to the research effort and, when invited into the work, can provide not just an evaluation but can also establish a more comfortable nonjudgmental conversation about the project/assignment. More official peer mentors (as in labs) can provide the same, given the time to develop trust and camaraderie. In both situations, the consultation pivots to collaboration and not criticism (Ervin, 2016). Collaborative feedback encourages student researchers to persist and to strive to improve the writing and the overall task.

Consulting with Advisor, Mentor, or Faculty Instructor

Advisors, mentors, and faculty instructors are available to provide student researchers with in-depth feedback on the work, especially if together they use the course/assignment or a scoring rubric. The purposes of these types of consultations can include (a) adequacy of resources, (b) quality of writing, and/or (c) clarity of sections of the work (e.g., the Discussion, Summary, and Conclusions).

A Cautious Reminder

Overall, feedback and opportunities to use that feedback help the researcher to "see" the work from another perspective, to make better informed decisions and to improve and enhance the work. However, to receive and use feedback to improve the quality of the work, researchers must develop a timeline/schedule that allocates time for this important input.

Step V. Dissemination: An Essential Part of the Research Process

Dissemination

Dissemination is an essential and required part of the research process: it refers to the process of sharing research findings not only with audiences of peers but also with a wider audience. It is essential for uptake and use of research findings and is crucial for the success and sustainability of practice-based research networks (PBRNs) in the long term. A high-quality review of the literature qualifies for presentation in both formal and informal settings.

In-Class Opportunities

Student researchers have an opportunity to (a) learn about communicating the information presented, (b) judge their work against external criteria, and (c) to identify peers with whom they can collaborate in the future. PowerPoint presentations or other presentation formats can serve this purpose.

School/Department Research Day Celebrations

Schools or departments provide opportunities for student researchers to present works in progress and to solicit feedback from faculty and peers on their topic. The benefits for students in these arenas include expanding their own network, improving their communications, and adding value to their new knowledge and capabilities. These forums are an important part of the process for feedback and metacognition to continually help students to refine their thinking processes.

Local/Regional/National Conferences

Conferences provide opportunities for a full demonstration of faculty-student scholarly collaboration where faculty teacher-scholars bring their original scholarship to a more public arena and include students as junior collaborators. This does not exclude student researchers from participating on their own at student conferences.

Conference presentations offer student researchers opportunities to experience the benefits of undergraduate research—*learning by doing*. In addition, student researchers can expand their network of peers and near-peers who are similarly engaged, become more knowledgeable on a topic in education and contribute to research in education, acquire a range of tools and competencies, all of which, with rehearsals and practice, add to their proficiency.

Conclusion

This chapter introduced the review of the literature as at the core of the research process and made clear the contribution of completing a literature review to a researcher's investigation and other academic endeavors. The chapter invited student researchers to a diligent and comprehensive investment in a step-by-step approach that has the potential to lead to a successful literature review and, at the same time, to contribute to the researchers' personal and academic development. Repetitions and continuing rehearsals of this literature review process set the academic and socioemotional foundation for students to be optimistic regarding the next steps of the research experience and to be convinced about learning by doing.

Notes

1 **Qualitative** research generates "textual data" (non-numerical). **Quantitative** research, on the contrary, produces "numerical data" or information that can

be converted into numbers. Often, some researchers utilize both approaches, referred to as mixed methods.

2 **LibGuides/Research Guides** is an easy-to-use content management system deployed at libraries worldwide. Librarians use them to curate knowledge, share information, organize class/subject-specific resources, and to create and manage websites.

3 **Inquiry** (-based **learning**) is a learning and **teaching approach** that emphasizes students' role in the learning process—asking questions, ideas, and observations. Instructors actively encourage students to share their thoughts and to respectfully challenge, test, and redefine ideas (John Dewey).

4 EBSCO*host* is an intuitive online research platform used by many institutions local, national, and worldwide. With its quality databases and search features, EBSCO*host* helps researchers find information needed immediately.

5 Boolean logic/operators are words such as "AND," "OR," and "NOT" that narrow or broaden the results of a search inquiry. Researchers use Boolean logic/operators to obtain more focused and productive results. The rules for applying Boolean logic/operators differ from database to database so it is recommended that you use the HELP option in the database to identify which rules apply.

References

Ames, C. (1992). Classroom: Goals, structures and student motivation. *Journal of Educational Psychology, 84*(3), 261–271.

Denney, A. S., & Tewksbury, R. (2013). How to write a literature review. *Journal of Criminal Justice Education, 24*(2), 218–234.

Dewey, J. (1938). *Experience and Education.* New York: MacMillan.

Dewey, J. (1991). Logic. The theory of inquiry. The Later works of John Dewey Vol. 12 Edited by Jo Ann Boydston (Carbondale & Edwardsville: Southern Illinois University Press).

Ervin, C. (2016). The peer perspective and undergraduate writing tutor research. *Praxis: A Writing Center Journal, 13*(2), 47–51.

Meulemans, N. Y., & Carr, A. (2012). Not at your service: Building genuine faculty-librarian partnerships. Reference Services Review, *41*(1), 80–90. https://doi.org/10.1108/00907321311300893

Piaget, J. (1936). *Origins of Intelligence in the Child.* London: Routledge & Kegan Paul.

Zorn, T., & Campbell, N. (2006). Improving the writing of literature reviews through a literature integration exercise. *Business Communication Quarterly, 69*(2), 172–183.

4 The Demands of Reading, Writing, and Thinking Like Researchers

Deborah L. Thompson

> Reading comprehension makes a full student; robust argument, a ready student; clear writing, an exact student; and thinking critically while engaging in the previous three, a prepared student.
>
> Sir Francis Bacon (paraphrased)

At one time, literacy was defined as the ability to read and write one's name. Such a definition is sufficient to describe the reading/writing abilities of most Americans from the late 19th to the mid-20th centuries, but with scientific, technological, medical, and educational advancements, accurate definitions of literacy require an inclusion of social context and cognition. A recent definition of literacy (2020) promoted by UNESCO best captures the current concept of literacy: "a **means** of identification, understanding, interpretation, creation, and communication in an increasingly digital, text-mediated, information-rich and fast-changing world. (https://en.unesco.org/themes/literacy)." Students must master all facets of literacy as they advance from preschool to 12th grade. As they enter college or other postsecondary programs, students are expected to be able to negotiate the complex assignments that are the foundation of college coursework. From first-year seminars to senior colloquia, undergraduates encounter a variety of texts: traditional hard- and soft-cover books, government documents, monographs, e-books and other digital fare, blogs, musical scores, magazines/journals, and social media posts. Each text is built on a specific foundation—a text structure. "Text structure" refers to the organizational features of a piece of text. These structures influence how much information students remember and understand after reading a selection. Also, a variety of factors influence students' comprehension, from a limited or lack of background knowledge of the topic to their failure to adjust to the type of text being read. For example, in shifting from reading fiction (narratives) to reading nonfiction, the internal structures can present barriers to comprehension.

A Brief Primer on Text Structure

Three basic structures of text—narrative, expository, and procedural—make up most of the reading materials students encounter throughout their school

DOI: 10.4324/9781003226475-4

and vocational careers. Narrative texts are stories and are the easiest to negotiate because humans exist in a universe of stories (e.g., explaining how the
dog ate the assignment due tomorrow, telling one's partner how the joint
bank account was overdrawn for the third week in a row, "fender bender?
What fender bender?" or creating an excuse for why the cat is on the kitchen
table licking the icing from the cake). Barbara Hardy (1968) stated that narratives (stories) engage our interests, curiosity, fears, tensions, expectations,
and sense of order; in other words, narrative is a primary act of mind (p. 5).
In school, narratives take different forms: novels, short stories, and plays. Although their content and complexity of themes, sentence structure, literary
devices, and vocabulary differ, in essence, *War and Peace* (Tolstoy, 2008) and
The Cat in the Hat (Geisel, 1957) have structural similarities; each has a beginning, middle, and end. As many English majors can attest, the difficulties
in reading narratives are often related to complex themes, sentence structure,
vocabulary density, and a multitude of literary devices.

Expository or nonfiction texts are also governed by their structures.
But where narratives usually have a beginning, middle, and end, the basic structures of expository texts vary: description, definition, sequences,
compare/contrast, cause and effect, and problem and solution. Being able
to recognize the different expository structures makes reading nonfiction
less difficult but still challenging. Common forms of expository texts are
textbooks, lab reports, government documents, research articles, and essays. Expository text structures may be difficult to comprehend, but they
come with internal support to help with comprehension: key words and
phrases such as *first, second, next, finally, while, like, unlike, because, nevertheless,
conclude,* and *propose*. Procedural texts give directions for doing something,
for example, a recipe or a science experiment. Most of the non-narrative
texts students read are a combination of expository and procedural texts.
A research article is usually a combination of expository and procedural
texts, but, in some cases, an article is a combination of narrative, expository, and procedural. The research article is the focus of the next section
of this chapter. The next section provides a guide to help undergraduates, specifically those in teacher education, read research articles with
understanding and to convert those understandings into written research
projects and presentations that will extend the content and pedagogical
knowledge they carry into their classrooms.

The Role of Research in Undergraduate
Teacher Education

Undergraduates in selected undergraduate majors have expectations of becoming researchers. Their programs of study include courses in research
methods, lessons in how to read research articles, classes on statistical analyses, and instructions on how to use academic writing to compose research
papers for dissemination. Such is the case with the physical and natural sciences. Research is a necessary component of physics, chemistry, and biology.

(Students studying to be secondary science teachers often participate in research in their content majors.) In the social sciences, disciplines such as psychology, anthropology, and sociology also have research components.

Conducting research is not as common among undergraduates who major in early childhood and elementary education unless they attend college in a state that requires Pre-K-6 teachers to have a second major in a subject area, such as biology, history, or math. In the college in which I taught, early childhood and elementary education majors often chose psychology as a second major (not considered a subject area major by the state but allowed if the preservice teacher did not teach above a certain grade). These students were well versed in research because they had to assist their professors in various labs and studies. The urban education majors also had a research component in their course of study, but other teacher education students were not exposed to research unless it was introduced through course-embedded assignments, independent studies, or honors requirements.

Some teacher education programs may include introductory research courses, but the majority of teacher education programs have courses that focus on classroom management, developing lesson plans, or how to teach a particular subject. Research can (and should) be a natural by-product of pedagogy-focused classes because so many of the assignments lend themselves to be reframed as strong foundations for research projects. It is not difficult to integrate research into courses if assignments are repurposed.

An initial step in educating fledgling undergraduate researchers is to help them learn how to read a research article. Research articles are not always easy to read and can be challenging, even to those who have the background knowledge and the requisite comprehension skills. Fortunately, learning how to read a research article and how to write a research report can be taught. The remainder of this section is a guide on how to read two different research articles. One is a highly technical piece on early literacy assessment and the other, a less technical research article on early literacy instruction. Although the research article topics are similar, the audience for each one is different (although the audiences may intersect, with readers interested in the content and research in both articles).

Analyzing a Technical Research Article

Technical research articles present problems to many readers, especially undergraduates, because such articles are written primarily for a specialized audience of researchers. Technical articles may contain statistical analyses presented in tabular form. Accessible research articles are legitimate research studies, but they are written for different reading consumers. Common statistical terms such as *raw scores, mean, median,* and *standard deviation* may remain in the main body of the article, with relevant technical statistics included in tables or appendices. The highly technical vocabulary and more impenetrable statistics have been removed or edited so that the reader does not have to try recall what different statistical terms mean, such as the difference between a *p* value and an *F* value. Unless the reader is keenly interested in statistical tests, not knowing the difference between *p* values and *F* values will not hinder the reader's comprehension of the article.

Research is separated into several methodological categories, with qualitative, quantitative, and mixed methods the most commonly used. The research reports/articles evolving from these methodologies include experimental studies, case studies, ethnographies, clinical trials (such as those for the Covid-19 vaccine), and meta-analyses (specialized literature reviews). Each type of research article requires a different reading approach. Shtulman (2018) recommended that to write a research article, academics should think of their writing tasks as "guiding a tour" that the reader joins to learn more about the research (p. 478). Using Shtulman's guided-tour strategy is a good way to read any research article. Each section of the research article serves as a marker. At the end of the guided tour, readers have a basic understanding of the research even though they may have had to negotiate their way through "unfamiliar theories and data" (p. 484).

The Guided Tour Begins—The *Reading Research Quarterly* Article

A literacy research article[1] was selected for the first analysis: "Assessing Inadequacies of the Observation Survey of Early Literacy." It is a technical article about the efficacy of using Marie Clay's *Observation Survey of Early Literacy Achievement* (OSELA; now in its fourth edition; originally published in 1993), an early literacy assessment tool with six subtests: letter recognition, concepts about print, text reading, phonemic awareness, reading vocabulary, and writing vocabulary. The 2017 article was selected because it was published in *Reading Research Quarterly*. *Reading Research Quarterly* is one of three journals published by the International Literacy Association. It is a premier literacy research journal. The OSELA is used to assess young children who are at risk for early literacy difficulties.

Marker 1: Abstract and Introduction

The first marker in this article is the abstract. An abstract, a compact summary of the article, is standard in research articles:

> The authors used nationally based, random sample data from three different years (2009–2010, 2011–2012, and 2014–2015) for nearly 20,000 first grade students (*n* = 9,760, 3,657, and 3,121, respectively) to examine long reported inadequacies of a commonly used early literacy assessment tool, the Observation Survey of Early Literacy Achievement (OSELA)[2]

[...] The authors maintain that the total score provides a more precise and efficient means of screening young students for reading failure and evaluating their progress over time. Implications for using the total score to make screening decisions and measure early reading progress are discussed.

(p. 51)

The introductory sentence reveals the breadth of the study (national), how many subjects were included, and how subjects were selected overall (20,000, random sampling) from three different years (2009–2010, 2011–2012, and 2014–2015), and the size of each randomized group (n = 9,760, n = 3,657, and n = 3,121). The lead sentence also provides the *why* or purpose of the research: to examine reported inadequacies of the widely used OSELA. The final two sentences present the findings of the research and implications for further research.

The introductory section of the article provides the context of the study. It is a review (a literature review) of all of the relevant research already conducted on the OSELA, including its limitations. From the findings of those studies, the researchers set the purpose of the study. In the review of the literature, the authors examined the definitive study of the OSELA published in 2004. The current study will use the 2004 study as the basis for research question 2 (discussed in the next section).

Marker 2: Purpose and Method

From the abstract, readers have been introduced to the purpose. What the extended purpose section does is provide the research questions that drive the study. The introduction provides the background for the research questions that are developed after a careful analysis of the existing relevant research. After synthesizing previous research studies about the OSELA, the authors developed three research questions:

1   Can the OSELA tasks be combined to create a unidimensional growth scale?
2   Does the growth scale overcome some of the obstacles of the six OSELA tasks, mainly the skewed distribution properties?
3   What is the predictive accuracy of the combined score? (p. 54)

By familiarizing themselves with the research questions, students will know what to look for as they read through the procedures, findings, and discussion. The authors report the results of three smaller studies in which they analyzed the different tasks in the OSELA. In the methodology section, the authors expand on how the random sampling was conducted.

Marker 3: Procedure and Findings

The procedure section is the most important section to researchers who wish to understand the scope of the studies. This section is also the most challenging to read for students new to research because this is where the types of statistics are used, and this article contains numerous graphs of the subjects' test scores. There are also tables. The graphs and tables are access or text features[3] that provide support for what is written in the main body of the article. For example, the reader can compare the results of three different testing periods for each period of the study by reading the histograms, or the reader can wade through the main body of the procedure section where the statistics can hinder the flow of reading. Tables also provide the reader with a better understanding of the technical language in the procedure section. Like the procedure section, the findings section helps other researchers determine the feasibility of replicate parts or all of this particular research study.

Marker 4: The End of the Guided Tour—The Discussion

In the discussion section, the researchers restate the goal of the research, the random sampling procedures used and a synthesis of the results of the different smaller studies, and finally how the findings of the studies can be used to improve the OSELA as a screening instrument.

The OSELA article was not written for a lay reader or undergraduate researcher. The article was chosen for this explanation because it is an excellent model of a quantitative research study. The reading demands shift with each section. The abstract, introduction, procedure, and discussion

Table 4.1 Text Structures in D'Agostino, Rodgers, and Mauck's (2017) Article

Article Section	Text Structures
Abstract	Description: The main features of the study are presented. This section activates any prior knowledge the reader may have of the research topic
Purpose and method	Description and sequence: The research questions set the sequence of the different studies. The method section is also descriptive with a mixture of procedural (how to) features
Procedure and findings	Much like the method section, the procedure section is a mixture of expository and procedural text. The findings section is descriptive, but it is challenging reading due to the presence of many statistical references and numerous tables and graphs
Discussion	Description: The researchers explain and extend their findings. They offer suggestions based on their findings for how to use the OSELA more efficiently

are easier to read because the text structures are more accessible. The findings present a bigger challenge because the text is interspersed with statistics. Table 4.1 reveals how the structures shift as the sections change.

The Second Guided Tour—*The Reading Teacher* Article

The second article analyzed is an accessible article that is also about early literacy: "As Easy as ABC? Teaching and Learning about Letters in Early Literacy" (Kaye & Lose, 2019).[4] This article was published in *The Reading Teacher*. *The Reading Teacher*, published by the International Literacy Association, is a leading practical research journal written for Pre-K–Grade 6 teachers, preservice teachers, teacher/researchers, and literacy researchers. Kaye and Lose apply known research on early reading and writing. A multi-aged K-1 classroom is used to highlight one teacher's "excellence" (the authors' term) in early literacy instruction.

Marker 1—Introduction and Purpose

As with the technical article, much of Marie Clay's early literacy research undergirds the research reported in this article. Unlike the technical article, the Kaye and Lose (2019) article does not begin with a research abstract. The single sentence at the beginning of the article serves as an *advanced organizer*—a literacy device that reminds readers what they already know about a topic and prepares them for any new information that will be encountered in the article. Although there is no extended explanation of the article, the introductory sentence reveals the intended audience: classroom teachers. How can busy teachers effectively support the development of young children's letter knowledge in the context of authentic reading and writing?

The purpose of the article (sequenced text) is embedded in the sixth paragraph of the seven-paragraph introduction:

> First, we provide an explanation of what is meant by the development of a literacy processing system. Second, we present an overview of important factors related to young students' emerging letter knowledge, including visual discrimination and the role of fast visual processing. Third, we show how a classroom teacher worked with individual learners in small-group and whole-class contexts in ways that built on their unique stores of letter knowledge and personal connections to letters while contributing to their self-efficacy.
>
> (p. 600)

Even though this article is reader-friendly, a reader's prior knowledge must include an understanding of literacy processing systems and factors relating to visual discrimination and letter knowledge. These specialized terms, familiar to a classroom teacher, will require undergraduates reading the article to use context (not always helpful) and access features and nonfiction structures. For example, the article has subheadings (an access feature) for the three specialized terms: letter knowledge, literacy processing, and visual discrimination. Undergraduates who have had experiences in Pre-K through first-grade classrooms will be more informed and will find that their background knowledge helps them comprehend the article more easily.

The nonfiction structures used in this article so far are description and definition: "Letter knowledge ... includes knowing the shape or form of letters, identifying letters by name, relating sounds to letters, forming letters (52 in English), and understanding the classification concept of 'letter'" (p. 601). The authors use description and definition to help inform readers who are unfamiliar with the terms *visual discrimination* and *literacy processing systems*.

Marker 2: Classroom Vignettes

One of the major features of most articles in *The Reading Teacher* is the classroom vignette. The vignettes focus on research findings as revealed through practical classroom applications in an exemplary classroom (or classrooms). Included in the vignette are the teacher's demonstrations of mini-lessons on letter knowledge, visual discrimination, and literacy processing. There are also figures of children's early attempts at writing, giving undergraduate readers visuals to add to their understanding of the concept of letter knowledge.

Classroom dialogue is also a part of each vignette. In the article's vignette, the dialogue reveals the interaction between teacher and students. The sections of dialogue are long enough to provide the reader with a demonstration of how a master teacher employs different strategies to nurture students' literacy development.

Marker 3: Access Features

The Reading Teacher article, unlike the *Reading Research Quarterly* article, has richer access features. As mentioned, the subheadings activate the reader's prior knowledge of early literacy development. Before the classroom vignette begins, there is a section of questions labeled "Pause and Ponder." Four bulleted questions in a mid-page text area are placed there to activate readers' prior knowledge. Although the questions are written for classroom teachers, they would help undergraduates focus on areas in the vignette that will help them answer questions that evolve from their reading. Other access features include illustrations (labeled as figures) of young children's early attempts at letter formation and connected writing. Children's letter knowledge through the manipulation of magnetic letters accompanies charts (also labeled as figures) that reveal their ability to identify letters of the alphabet. Ending the article is a set of recommended actions for the classroom teacher. The audience for the "Pause and Ponder" feature and "Take Action" feature is in the Pre-K-12 classroom, but this should not preclude undergraduate college students from using them to extend their knowledge of early literacy development relative to letter knowledge, literacy processing, and visual discrimination.

Expository or Narrative?

Another reason *The Reading Teacher* article is easier to comprehend is that it mimics a narrative structure. In recent years, authors of commercial nonfiction works have transformed traditional stilted expository writing (think *textbooks*) to works that read like narratives, for example, Larson's *The Devil in the White City* (2004) or Wilkerson's *The Warmth of Other Suns* (2010). Much like well-written fiction, the works by Larson and Wilkerson and other exemplary nonfiction writers draw readers in and rivet their attention until the end.

Newkirk (2012) noted, much as Hardy did, that humans have a craving for narrative. Interestingly enough, the transformation from stilted academic texts to readable text has also infused academic writing. For example, there is the use of first-person pronouns, a nonstarter in formal essays written in some high school and college courses. The *Reading Research Quarterly* article with three authors and *The Reading Teacher* article with two authors incorporated the use of "we." That shift alone makes reading an unfamiliar piece easier. *The Reading Teacher* article also did not contain as much technical vocabulary as did the *Reading Research Quarterly*

Table 4.2 A Structural Comparison of the Articles

Attribute	The Reading Research Quarterly Article	The Reading Teacher Article
Text type	Expository/procedural	Expository/narrative nonfiction
Text structures	Description, definition, sequence	Description, definition
Access features	Abstract, statistical tables, histograms, research subheadings—purpose, method, data collection, procedure, findings, discussion	Advanced organizer, subheadings, questions, figures in the form of children's writing, charts of children's letter knowledge
Audience	Researchers, advanced graduate students, literacy professors, literacy coaches, classroom teachers	Graduate students, classroom teachers, upper-level undergraduates

article. The accessible writing has several descriptors including "narrative nonfiction." Narrative nonfiction is an oxymoron to be sure, but it clearly describes the accessibility of the more recent articles in some academic fields. Although *The Reading Teacher* article does not compare to reading Larson or Wilkerson, the article's construction, narrative patterns, and technical vocabulary make it an excellent vehicle to teach undergraduates to read like researchers. Table 4.2 shows how each article is a composite of a variety of text types.

Acts of Cognition or Thinking and Writing Like Researchers

"Thinking like a researcher" is the cognitive environment in which "writing like a researcher" exists. Please note that "writing like a researcher" should not be confused with writing a research report (covered in a later chapter of this book). Writing like a researcher is an act of cognition. Writing a research report is a product of that cognitive act. To write like a researcher requires knowing the basic tenets of research writing: knowledge of the research genre, an adequate grasp of academic writing and specialized vocabulary, knowledge of the subject matter, and knowledge of audience.

Writing Like a Researcher and the Challenges of Academic Writing

When researchers have their papers accepted for publication in peer-reviewed journals or for presenting at a major conference, it is a sign that they have mastered the intricacies of the "academic writing." Just what is academic writing? Wolsey, Lapp, and Fisher (2012) describe academic writing as a robustly written discourse in which the writer conveys an in-depth knowledge of discipline-specific concepts (e.g., how heuristic language is used by kindergarten students, or what are the effects of deforestation on climate change?). Akkaya and Aydin's (2018) definition of academic writing is even more specific: writing that serves as a vehicle for "sharing original research with other scholars" (p. 128). Rahimivanda and Kuhi (2014) posit that academic writing is "a collective social practice in the academic discourse community" (p. 1493). All three definitions connect writing to the social contexts of discourse communities that exist in the academy: teacher/scholar/researcher. These discourse communities are the fertile fields student researchers enter as they learn to write like researchers—where they move from compositions written solely to satisfy a single professor to writing purposeful compositions rooted in the authentic world of undergraduate research for broad and informed audiences.

From Writing for an Audience of One to an Audience of Many

Undergraduates enter college "highly skilled" in writing for an audience of one: their high school teachers. They also have experience writing in one of two common formats: the "term paper" or the all-purpose five-paragraph essay. In many of their college classes there is a continuation of these solo writing performances, for example, book critiques written for the history or English professor or journal entries ostensibly written for oneself, but actually written for professors. Writing the results of a research study for dissemination requires undergraduates to shift from trying to satisfy that solo audience to writing for a wide-ranging audience of peers, mentors, and other interested parties. Because format (e.g., journal articles, book reviews, conference presentations) and audience influence vocabulary use, sentence construction, and other conventions of academic writing, undergraduate researchers must have a deep understanding of the disciplinary concepts in which their research is anchored, and they must know the standard rules governing the format (e.g., article, paper presentation, or poster presentation) in which their research will be shared. As Medeiros and Kinney (2020) noted,

> [T]he rules and language for writing change depending on type of writing (genre) and intended audience. Psychologists writing for psychologists, for example, will likely take a different approach than if writing for biologists. In the former, they might assume shared understanding of key concepts and make technical word choices that "insiders" would understand. In the latter, they might provide a more comprehensive explanation of key ideas that might not be well known outside their particular discipline or choose words that are more inclusive to "outsiders."
>
> (p. 794)

Learning to write like researchers means that undergraduates must become proficient in writing for interested, informed audiences (insiders) as well as interested, uninformed audiences (outsiders).

Successful researchers know their audiences and the written formats necessary to disseminate their research findings. That D'Agostino, Rodgers, and Mauck (2017) had their research published in a leading literacy research journal meant that they had control of each principle of academic writing: (a) the format/genre: research study, the vocabulary, sentence structure and other conventions of said format, and the audience; and (b) informed peers: advanced doctoral students and seasoned literacy researchers and teachers. *The Reading Teacher* article by Kaye and Lose reflected that they too mastered the principles of academic writing, but they adjusted their sentence structure and vocabulary for a different audience reading with a different purpose. *The Reading Teacher* article sheds the statistics and technical explanations found in the *Reading Research Quarterly* article—not because those items are unimportant, but because they are not needed for the purposes of understanding the research highlighted in *The Reading Teacher* article. Research articles published in journals such as *The Reading Teacher* are written for practitioners who may not have the time or inclination to read a dense research article, even if they are familiar with (and many are) Clay's assessments. Undergraduate researchers need models of accessibly written research. Practitioner articles are appropriate models for teaching undergraduate researchers how to think and write like researchers because such articles are written by outstanding teacher/researchers who can provide avenues into the thinking patterns of good researchers.

Other Challenges of Writing Like Researchers

Numerous researchers have written about the challenges academic writing poses for native English speakers (L1) and nonnative speakers (L2) (Campbell, 2019; Hyland, 2002; Karunarathna, 2020). Arcane rules, holdovers from a more formal era of writing, are still speedbumps in composing academic writing (e.g., objectivity, writing in third person, and avoiding using the personal pronoun "I"). Such rules, Hyland (2002) stated, are based on the erroneous belief that "academic research is purely empirical and objective." These acts of writer concealment are what Gertz (as cited in Hyland, 2002) called "author-evacuated prose" (p. 1095). Such concealment may satisfy objectivity on some levels, but overall, "author-evacuated" prose is often stilted and uninspiring.

Another recent challenge to composing in the academic writing sphere relates to gender-fair usage. Authors of a certain age (this author included) remember that one rule of objectivity was the use of the universal or generic "he." Currently, the use of pronouns he, she, he/she has given way for what Stromborn (2020) calls "epicene pronouns or third-person pronouns of indeterminant gender" (p. 193). Currently, the most commonly used epicene pronoun is the "nongendered singular they." Typical rules of reference—the singular noun "student" or "researcher" and the singular antecedent "he"—are no longer viable. For example, in times past, the following was an allowable sentence: "The researcher double-checked his notes to ensure a successful experiment." A more recent iteration of this sentence would have substituted "his/her" for "his." Using gender-fair usage rules, the same sentence reads "The *researcher* double-checked *their* notes to ensure a successful experiment." The epicene pronoun—the singular "their"—denotes no particular gender. Format changes below from American Psychological Association

(APA) and National Council of Teachers for English (NCTE) reveal the current rules for use of pronouns:

APA Style Manual, 7th Ed.

Do not use the generic "he" or "he or she" to refer to a generic person; instead, rewrite the sentence or use the singular "they." When writing about a known individual, use that person's identified pronouns. https://apastyle.apa.org/style-grammar-guidelines/bias-free-language/gender

NCTE Rules on Gender and Language (2018)
https://ncte.org/statement/genderfairuseoflang/

- Avoid using *he* as a universal pronoun; likewise, avoid using binary alternatives such as *he/she, he or she*, or *(s)he*.
- The pronoun *they* is appropriate to use in writing when referring to singular antecedents, including when writing for publication.
- Unless the gender of a singular personal antecedent is otherwise specified, use the gender-neutral singular pronouns *they, them, their*, and *theirs*.
- *Are* is the present-tense verb for the singular pronoun *they*, just as *are* is the present-tense verb for the singular pronoun *you*.

Such rules can be internalized through an active undergraduate research program that provides students unlimited opportunities to write their research findings for different audiences.

Returning to Shtulman's analogy (2018), to write an accessible research report/article, the writer should think of guiding a tour—the task of writing for a wide audience includes avoiding jargon, not providing too much information (avoiding what Shtulman calls the "curse of knowledge"), and avoiding ambiguity. Shtulman advises writing crisply, using vocabulary appropriate for the level of the reader and avoiding stilted academic vocabulary (p. 480). Being conversational in writing is not the same as being informal. The following example from the conclusion of Kaye and Lose's *Reading Teacher* article is a good example of how skilled writers have synthesized the current rules governing academic language. The writing flows, is not stilted, and is conversational but not informal:

Clearly, letter learning for young students is not as easy as one may think. It is exceedingly complex, and even more so for particular students. Control of letter knowledge evolves over time (not in alphabetical order or by a letter per week) and varies considerably from student to student, yet it is essential to the development of an early literacy processing system.

(Kaye & Lose, 2019, p. 609)

Using the RAFT Strategy to Write Like a Researcher

One way to help undergraduates write like researchers is to give them a structure in which they have to use different formats to reach different audiences. An effective structured strategy to help students to write like researchers is the RAFT strategy. Carol Santa introduced the interdisciplinary RAFT strategy in 1988. RAFT is an acronym that stands for **R**ole, **A**udience, **F**ormat, and **T**opic. RAFT has been studied across the curricular spectrum and has been found to (a) help secondary ESL (English as Second Language) students write effective argumentative and persuasive essays (Kabigting, 2020); (b) help students in science classes connect prior and new information to become more environmentally literate (Groenke & Puckett, 2006); (c) help gifted students with learning disabilities learn and practice the different roles of writers (Yssel, Adams, Clarke, & Jones, 2014); (d) help middle-school teachers incorporate writing into math classes as recommended by the National Council of Teachers of Mathematics (Gunter, 2016); and (e) serve as an authentic and effective assessment tool in secondary physical science classes (Dani, Hallman-Thrasher, & Litchfield, 2018). Using RAFT allows students to don the "mantle of the expert or the one who knows or is the expert in a specific area of human knowledge" (Heathcote & Herbert, 1985, p. 173). Although Heathcote and Herbert's focus was on drama as a tool of instruction, RAFT is not unlike a dramatization in which undergraduate researchers are the experts disseminating (or performing) their research for various audiences. RAFT helps student researchers to use writing as a way to show depth of understanding of their research and the processes needed to arrive at the conclusions for dissemination to wider

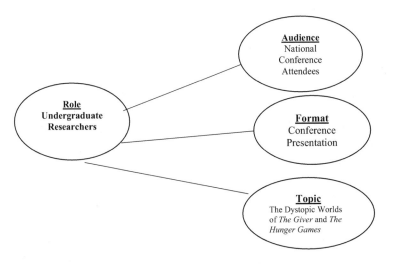

Figure 4.1 RAFT for a National Conference Presentation.

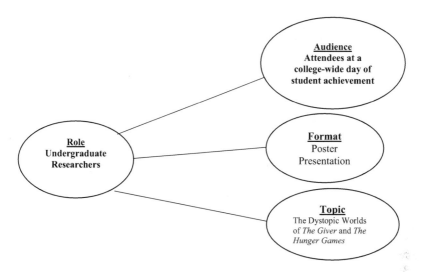

Figure 4.2 RAFT for a Campus-Wide Student Research Presentation.

informed and lay audiences. Figures 4.1 and 4.2 show how changing roles provided two students two ways to present the results of their independent study on two dystopian adolescent novels, *The Giver* (Lowry, 1993) and *The Hunger Games* (Collins, 2008).

Conclusion

Undergraduate research provides pathways of opportunities for pre-service teachers to become members of the discourse community of teacher-scholar researchers. In learning to read, write, and think like researchers, students can successfully conduct research and present their findings to likeminded peers and mentors. Undergraduates who engage in research reveal their deep understandings of the disciplinary concepts that inform their areas of study. When writing for their discourse communities, undergraduate researchers reveal their mastery of the standard rules governing the written formats of research. Participating in undergraduate research advantages all students who engage in research over those who do not (Bowman & Holmes, 2018). This holds true across ethnic and racial groups and across collegiate majors beyond those majors that traditionally have research components such as the STEM (science, technology, engineering, and mathematics) majors (Baron, Brown, Cumming, & Mengeling, 2020).

The more undergraduates read accessible research, conduct research, and present the results, the more students will see that teacher education is a field that naturally thrives on research. Undergraduate teacher educators belong in the discourse communities of teacher-scholar researchers. Being members of such communities prepares them to teach innovatively in these challenging times. Sir Francis Bacon may not have had undergraduate research in mind, but he would undoubtedly agree that undergraduate research, with its robust arguments, exceptional academic writing, and critical thinking, creates the environment for full, ready, exact, and prepared teacher education majors.

Notes

1 The author thanks Dr. Jerome V. D'Agostino and Dr. Emily Rodgers of The Ohio State University, Columbus for permission to use their article in this chapter.
2 Ellipses indicate deleted text deemed unnecessary for the analysis of the article.
3 Access or text features are sections of the text not within the main body of an article or chapter. For example, chapter headings, graphic organizers, captions and pictures, end-of-chapter questions, tables, and sidebars.
4 Kaye, E. L., & Lose, M. K. (2019). As easy as A-B-C? Teaching and learning about letters in early literacy. *The Reading Teacher, 72*(5), 599–610. Open-access article.

References

Akkaya, A., & Aydin, G. (2018). Academics' views on the characteristics of academic writing. *Educational Policy Analysis and Strategic Research, 13*(2), 128–160.

American Psychological Association. (2020). *Publication manual of the American Psychological Association*, 7th ed. Washington, DC: APA.

Baron, S. I., Brown, P., Cumming, T., & Mengeling, M. (2020). The impact of undergraduate research and student characteristics on student success metrics at an urban minority serving, commuter, public institution. *Journal of Scholarship of Teaching and Learning, 20*(1), 85–104.

Bowman, N. A., & Holmes, J. M. (2018). Getting off to a good start? First-year undergraduate research experiences and student outcomes. *Higher Education (00181560), 76*(1), 17–33. https://ezproxy.tcnj.edu:2083/10.1007/s10734-0191-4

Buddhima Karunarathna, J. A. M. (2020). Improving the use of language hedges in academic writing through reading journal articles. *Advances in Language Studies, 11*(3), 17–23. http://dx.doi.org/10.7575/aiac.alls.v.11n.3p.17

Campbell, M. (2019). Teaching academic writing in higher education. *Education Quarterly Reviews, 2*(3), 608–614. http://dx.doi.org/10.31014/aior.1993.02.03.92

Collins, S. (2008). *The hunger games.* New York: Scholastic.

D'Agostino, J. V., Rodgers, E., & Mauck, S. (2017). Addressing the inadequacies of the observation survey of early literacy achievement. *Reading Research Quarterly, 53*(1), 51–69.

Dani, D., Hallman-Thrasher, A., & Litchfield, E. (2018). Creative assessments. *Science Teacher, 85*(5), 46–53.

Geisel, T. Dr. Seuss. (1957). *The cat in the hat.* New York: Random House

Groenke, S. L., & Puckett, R. (2006). Becoming environmentally literate citizens. *Science Teacher, 73*(8), 22–27.

Gunter, M. D. (2016). Riding the RAFT. *Mathematics Teaching in the Middle School*, *22*(3), 172–175.

Hardy, B. (1968). Towards a poetics of fiction: An approach through narrative. *Novel: A Forum on Fiction*, *2*(1), 5–14.

Heathcote, D., & Herbert, P. (1985). A drama of learning: Mantle of the expert. *Theory into Practice*, *24*(3), 173–180.

Hyland, K. (2002). Authority and invisibility: Authorial identity in academic writing. *Journal of Pragmatics*, *34*(8), 1091–1112. https://ezproxy.tcnj.edu:2083/10.1016/S0378-2166(02)00035-8

Kabigting, R. P. (2020). Utilizing the RAFT strategy: Its effects on the writing performance of Filipino ESL learners. *Journal of English Teaching*, *6*(3), 173–182.

Kaye, E. L., & Lose, M. K. (2019). As easy as A-B-C? Teaching and learning about letters in early literacy. *The Reading Teacher*, *72*(5), 599–610.

Larson, E. (2004). *The devil in the White city: Murder, magic, and madness at the fair that changed America*. New York: Vintage.

Lowry, L. (1993). *The giver*. Boston, MA: Houghton Mifflin Harcourt.

Medeiros, K. de., & Kinney, J. M. (2020). Writing like a gerontologist for *The Gerontologist*. *Gerontologist*, *60*(5), 793–796. https://ezproxy.tcnj.edu.2083/10.1093/geront/gnaa060

National Council of Teachers of English. (2018). *NCTE statement on gender and language*. https://ncte.org/statement/genderfairuseoflang/

Newkirk, T. (2012). How we really comprehend nonfiction. *Educational Leadership*, *69*(6), 28–32.

Rahimivanda, M., & Kuhi, D. (2014). An exploration of discoursal construction of identity in academic writing. *Procedia – Social and Behavioral Sciences*, *98*, 1492–1501.

Santa, C. M. (1988). *Content reading including study systems: Reading, writing and studying across the curriculum*. Dubuque, IA: Kendall/Hunt Publishing.

Shtulman, A. (2018). Communicating developmental science to nonscientists, or how to write something even your family will want to read. *Journal of Cognition and Development*, *19*(5), 477–485.

Stromborn, C. (2020). Gendering in open access research articles: The role of epicene pronouns. *English for Specific Purposes: An International Journal*, *60*, 193–204.

Tolstoy, L. (2008). *War and peace* (Vintage Classic Ed.). New York: Vintage.

UNESCO. (2020). *Literacy defined*. https://en.unesco.org/themes/literacy.

Wilkerson, I. (2010). *The warmth of other suns: The epic story of America's great migration*. New York: Random House.

Wolsey, T. D., Lapp, D., & Fisher, D. (2012). Students' and teachers' perceptions: An inquiry into academic writing. *Journal of Adolescent & Adult Literacy*, *55*(8), 714–724. https://ezproxy.tcnj.edu.2083/10.1002/JAAL.00086

Yssel, N., Adams, C., Clarke, L. S., & Jones, R. (2014). Applying an RTI model for students with learning disabilities who are gifted. *Teaching Exceptional Children*, *46*(3), 42–52.

5 Technology

The All-Purpose Research Tool for Discovery, Organization, and Collaboration

Judi Puritz Cook

As colleges and universities evolve to embrace digital learning environments for instruction, one area that is poised to benefit from this paradigm shift is the realm of undergraduate research. Online resources and tools open up a wealth of possibilities for undergraduate students and the research projects they develop. And yet, the plethora of options and different interfaces can sometimes be overwhelming, and, without a clear plan, it is possible to miss out on tools that could help strengthen, deepen, and improve the work. This chapter aims to shed light on the right tools for the right tasks, with the goal of helping you evaluate your options and make strategic choices in the use of online tools for research. Additional suggestions for connecting to mentors, scholarly communities, and training sites will also be addressed.

Practical solutions for leveraging digital tools in the design, implementation, evaluation, and distribution of scholarship can be of value to any researcher, but particularly useful to an undergraduate who is new to the process. This chapter will focus specifically on digital tools for discovery, organization, and collaboration, while also offering direction for students interested in tools related to data collection and analysis. Much of what is included in this chapter can be integrated in the other parts of this book. For example, guidance here in strategies for improving database searches will dovetail with Suzanne Lindt and Emily Rutherford's advice on creating literature reviews. Similarly, Catherine Packer-Williams' chapter on building a research community may be enhanced by the concepts for collaboration covered here. The goal of this chapter is to help you infuse technology-enhanced solutions in all aspects of the research process.

This chapter highlights digital skills, concepts, and capabilities that can enhance any undergraduate research projects across a range of disciplines, but it specifically targets students engaged in research in the field of education. The digital literacy practices presented may have application in other areas of academic life and academic disciplines as well. It is critical to know, however, that each discipline approaches undergraduate research differently, and within the realm of possibilities the specific methods and approaches (i.e., qualitative vs. quantitative), some disciplines may lend themselves to specific technologies while rendering others less relevant. In

DOI: 10.4324/9781003226475-5

expanding an understanding of those specific approaches, you will have a better ability to evaluate the strategies presented here as more useful or less useful, and for the later, you will be able to conduct your own searches to find best practices for undergraduate research in specific disciplines. Knowledge of transferable technology skills can also benefit other aspects of discovery outside of academia.

Discovery and Digital Literacy: Why the Library Should Be Your First Stop

Digital literacy and information literacy go hand in hand, and today's undergraduate students require aspects of both in their academic toolkit. The American Library Association defines digital literacy as "...the ability to use information and communication technologies to find, evaluate, create, and communicate information, requiring both cognitive and technical skills" (Digital Literacy, 2019, p. 1). It takes the concept of information literacy and adds in the collaborative and social nature of today's networked systems. Knowledge of what is possible and pragmatic from a digital literacy standpoint will inform a research trajectory and save time—as long as there is an investment of time up front, getting familiar with basic strategies that will set you up for success. Good habits can go a long way, and when the technology evolves, those who understand the underlying principles will be better equipped for future advances. Just being born in a technology-rich environment does not guarantee a deep understanding of use and application of technological solutions.

And yet, research on digital literacy often calls attention to the assumption that all undergraduates born in the last two decades are automatically tech-savvy (Hargittai & Walejko, 2008; Losh, 2021; Vaidhyanathan, 2008). Assuming all students are tech-savvy is problematic, as being familiar with contemporary, digital tools for living does not necessarily correlate with an understanding of how tools work, or how best to select a digital tool for academic work. In the case of discovery work, you can benefit from identifying targeted tools and techniques for searching. These skills will be useful at the front end of any research project as you set out to make sense of an existing landscape.

Examinations of information-seeking practices of undergraduates (Vinyard, Mullally, & Colvin, 2017) identify a "do-it-yourself" approach to discovery work. According to Perruso (2016), the majority of first-year students begin the discovery process with Google or a similar search engine. That strategy is not without merit (later sections of this chapter will discuss best practices for discovery with Google and Wikipedia) but skips over valuable, free resources from the library that could provide a starting point with greater depth and breadth. Despite the widespread availability of research librarians on college campuses, not all students head to the library first. In fact, Miller and Murillo (2012) found that students were more likely to ask their instructors and their friends for help over librarians. Faculty may find this baffling, as many bring in librarians as guest speakers or share LibGuides with students with the understanding that students will utilize the instruction. So why are undergraduate students reluctant to ask a librarian for help or explore the library databases as a starting point in the process? Convenience may be a major factor in this practice (Connaway, Dickey, & Radford, 2011; Vondracek, 2007). Google is a familiar tool that already plays a central role in the lives of most people. Google searches use natural language search, which allows for phrasing of searches in everyday language. In contrast, library databases tend to rely on Boolean search, with keyword terms, connectors (and, or, not), truncation, and proximity operators.

While library websites are different, they face similar limitations if Google is the comparison interface. According to Kirkwood (2011), part of the challenge may be the nature of the library interfaces, with their maze of databases and lack of global discovery options. Finding trusted sources can be difficult and time-consuming, regardless of discovery tools employed (Kirkwood, 2011). This situation is evolving, however. Many academic libraries are reimagining their search options to provide greater ease of use and navigation. More natural language searches are yielding productive results, often right from the library home page.

Taking advantage of the library begins with making connection with a reference librarian. Reference librarians are ready to help individual students at any stage of the discovery process, and these interactions can happen in person or remotely. Reference librarians can also be subject-matter experts, armed with targeted options to get you what you need from the library. If something is not available electronically, many academic libraries offer interlibrary loan and/or document delivery services to get you articles or even whole chapters of print publications scanned and emailed to you. Partnering with a librarian is a best practice that will yield countless benefits for you, and all you have to do is ask for help—in the physical library at the reference desk, or online through your library's website. Chat options can be particularly helpful when you are short on time and need a little guidance. For more in-depth assistance, arrange for a one-on-one meeting.

A second strategy for success is to think beyond just *your* library. Reference librarians around the globe prepare LibGuides in a range of disciplines—curated content that can lead you to resources that will help you with your discovery efforts. The LibGuides tool is service provided by the company Spring Share, and over 130,000 librarians in 82 countries use the service to provide curated materials (Springshare, n.d.). To find LibGuides, do a Google search with the keywords Libguides and "teacher education"; you'll find librarian-curated contents from other universities to help fine-tune your approach. Conducting research in another discipline? Swap out "teacher education" for any field you may study, and you'll find yourself with top recommendations from librarians.

A third suggestion is to familiarize yourself with advanced search options within databases such as Education Resources Information Center (ERIC), or whatever database you are using. While searching, employ Boolean search terms such as AND, OR, and NOT to take advantage of targeted search strings. Employ quotation marks to search for phrases. Limit your search by fields to specifically examine your keywords in select areas, such as the title of articles. If you require scholarly, academic sources, look for any limiters to check off for peer-reviewed sources. And most important: familiarize yourself with the tools for saving or returning to any articles that you find, such as Permalink. All of your hard work will go to waste if you don't have an organized method of keeping track of your progress. Each record you find will contain a range of tools for exporting, downloading, printing, sharing, linking, and citing your findings. A word of caution about computer-generated citations: they are a great starting point, but often contain small errors that need to be corrected. So, whether or not you are following APA, MLA, Chicago, or some other style, be sure to double-check the entries for accuracy. It is up to you to ensure that your citations follow the style you may be asked to use.

What about Google and Wikipedia? Todorinova (2015) found that many undergraduates use Wikipedia to get background information on a topic, but they stay away from it as a serious source for discovery. While you might not want to cite Wikipedia as a source, you can use it to find information and apply your own digital literacy skills to evaluate the credibility of those sources (Purdue Writing Lab, n.d.). If the Wikipedia references meet standards for quality—judged by the source's credibility, the author's expertise, and so on—you can locate the references and review the content first-hand. In this manner, you may discover quality materials that just need a more discerning eye to evaluate. As Tondorinova suggests, this practice might be a useful way to integrate digital literacy, as it encourages students to critically examine Wikipedia and perhaps even get involved in the creation and editing of Wikipedia pages. In considering curated, crowd-sourced content found on Wikipedia, one might imagine it similar to a LibGuide—with the need for greater scrutiny to ensure the sources are appropriate and useful for your own scholarly endeavors.

Google (Google Scholar in particular) has its place and can be a pathway to discovering scholarly publications as well. Unlike general Google searches, which span all that is searchable on the Internet, Google Scholar limits results to academic sources (About Google Scholar, n.d.). Google advertises itself as a "one-stop shop" for discovery, designed to help you "stand on the shoulders of giants." But the reality is that if you only use Google Scholar you will miss out on other articles that could be waiting for you in the library's databases. It may seem tedious to put in a request for interlibrary loan, or to physically go to the stacks and pull a book off the shelf, but Google simply cannot replace a good, deep dive into a library's full resources. That said, Google *can* yield results that are useful, albeit not comprehensive. If you use Google Scholar and cannot access a full text for an article of interest, log in to your college's Google apps account and try the link again; in many cases, that will connect you directly to the library's database where you can get the full text. Alternatively, make a note of the article's details and try a search for full text through the library's databases directly. If it isn't available, put in an inter-library loan request. The extra steps you take to get to the source will be worth it.

Organization and Planning: How Technology Can Streamline Your Research Process

Like any large-scale project, research endeavors benefit from a clear work-flow and general plan. If you print out articles and don't keep track of citations, or take notes but don't provide enough details to help you properly cite your sources when you write, you may add on extra hours of work trying to undo the problems that can arise from being disorganized. Everyone has their own style for this type of work, so suggestions presented here are just one approach. Choose whatever works best for you, but keep in mind you will save time and possibly increase your productivity if you adopt a few of these strategies.

First, keep track of your citations as you find them with reference management software. Also known as bibliographic software, there are a number of tools to assist you in this important work, and their availability may vary depending on your university. For example, some universities will provide free access to software such as EndNote or Refworks. If you write inside Google Docs, the add-on EasyBib can give you a simple tool for putting citations directly into your papers in styles such as MLA, APA, Chicago, and more. The same caveat mentioned earlier applies, though; computer-generated tools for citations may be close to correct but often require you to fix minor errors in order to truly meet the requirements of your style format. Always examine the citations for errors and make corrections as needed. If you are not sure, go directly to the webpage for the style guide you are looking to follow. You'll be able to see examples that cover almost any scenario.

A second strategy is saving PDF versions of all articles you are considering for use in your research project. As you save the articles, rename the files so that when you look at the collection later you will recognize the file (e.g., include the article title, the author's name, and a date). At the start of your discovery phase, it may not be 100 percent clear which articles will be of value to you, and the ability to return to certain items will be beneficial. If you read on the screen, use bookmarks, notes, and digital highlighters to keep track of salient information in your articles. If you like the tactility of paper, print your articles and mark them up manually. As you find suitable materials for direct or indirect quotes, keep track in a document you create that makes note of the difference between a direct quote and something you've rewritten in your own words. Include the author's name and the year of publication. If it is a direct quote, include the page number. All of these details will speed things along when you begin writing. They will also protect you from accidentally plagiarizing.

Organization is generally helpful to any research project, but so too is the need to be thorough. A third recommendation is to stay on the lookout for great sources, using the already curated lists on the reference pages of the articles you have discovered. Take the time to review the reference pages for those sources. You may need to track down additional articles based on your preliminary work. If you notice a particular source that is cited in multiple places, it may be an important foundational resource. Whenever possible, find the original source or seminal piece of work that best contributes to your own project. In this way, you will more accurately "stand on the shoulders of giants."

All of the above steps take time, and none of it can happen overnight. For this reason, a critical step in the research process is developing a timeline. Work backwards from the date in which you need to have your work completed. Add a reasonable amount of time for drafts, outline creation, revisions, and searching. If you need to adjust your timeline, make sure you give yourself a buffer so that you can enjoy the work and not feel stressed by the pressure to finish on a tight deadline. If you are not hitting your target dates for the various parts of your paper, consult with someone who can help you before things get too out of hand. A faculty mentor may be able to help you strategize a more realistic timeline and provide for guidance based on what you have already accomplished.

Finding a Mentor

Undergraduate research is "an inquiry or investigation conducted by an undergraduate student that makes an original intellectual or creative contribution to the discipline" (Council on Undergraduate Research, n.d.). As you explore the opportunities to engage with other scholars, remember that you, even as an undergraduate, are also a scholar. Your intellectual contributions to your discipline have value. The work you do at the undergraduate level can be just as impactful as the work of those who have considerably more years of schooling or publications. That said, there is a great deal that can be learned from someone who has been in your shoes as an undergraduate and has gone on to do independent scholarship. Finding a mentor is an important step, as you will benefit from having an ally with experience and knowledge to guide you.

There are several steps you can take to distinguish your work and learn more about the process and preparation all scholars take in order to earn recognition and even get published. For some undergraduate students, this could be in the form of independent scholarship (e.g., you conduct a research project and write a paper that you submit to a conference or journal). More commonly, this work happens in concert with support and supervision of a faculty mentor, where there may be principal investigators (faculty or graduate students) and as an undergraduate you learn from helping with specific research tasks. To find a mentor, look around your campus and get a sense for what kind of research projects are being conducted by your faculty. The level of exposure you have to researchers on your campus will be determined by your program of study as well as your university's commitment to scholarship. If you find a faculty member who is conducting research you find interesting, do not be shy. Inquire about formal or informal ways you could get involved.

Formal opportunities may come in the form of programs specifically designed to pair students and faculty in research endeavors. For example, undergraduate students at The College of New Jersey can apply for the Mentored Undergraduate Summer Experience (MUSE), where students live on campus in the summer and conduct research in collaboration with faculty. The program funds research stipends and housing for the students who are accepted. Similar programs at other universities exist to cultivate the mentoring of students by faculty scholars. If you are not sure what's available at your campus, do some exploring. There may be opportunities that have not been on your radar. If you do not see anything like MUSE on your campus, consider something more informal. Approach your individual instructors and engage them in conversation about their research pursuits. Find out what sparks their passion about their field of study and how they go about participating in discipline-specific conversations about scholarship. Perhaps they would be willing to bring you in on a future project. See where you might be able to get involved.

Community, Collaboration, and Diversity of Thought: Ways to Leverage Connections

Given the social and collaborative elements embedded in the definition of digital literacy, it is no surprise that a technology-enhanced research plan would involve opportunities for collaboration, discussion, and interaction. If you are conducting independent research for an undergraduate class, that work does not need to happen in isolation. Similarly, group work can leverage technology in important ways, leading to greater accountability, greater diversity of thought, and less reliance on physical places or times for meeting. Opportunities exist for you to connect with other researchers who share an interest in your topic, or who might be willing to preview your work in progress. You can seek out professional groups on social media, where access to a large number of people with an interest in your discipline may be available to answer questions. Academic discussion boards and interest groups provide access to a wide range of perspectives. Cloud computing allows for document sharing and group editing.

For example, sharing a Google Doc provides for an expedient way to get feedback, co-author a document, or share progress. Participants can have access at a range of levels, depending on the need to edit, comment, or just view. A document history provides a way to view earlier iterations of a document and restore to a previous version as needed. Tags alert participants to changes and when an action is needed. Through the use of collaborative writing tools, undergraduate students can integrate feedback more immediately. Cloud tools eliminate the need to distribute documents via email and instead allow for real-time updates visible to anyone with access to the document. Be sure to back up your documents to a physical drive, as your research should be protected. Back up all PDFs and articles to ensure you always have access to what you need.

If you would like to join a community of scholars for conversations about your topic, one option is to explore the social media presence of any academic organizations affiliated with your discipline. For example, the National Association of Childhood Teacher Educators (NAECTE) maintains a public Facebook group for conversations and sharing of information related to their work. Twitter, Instagram, Pinterest, LinkedIn, YouTube, and other social media platforms may also serve as vehicles to put you in touch with scholars with whom you could connect and engage. Authors of articles you find central to your research may be active in ResearchGate.net, which may help you discover other researchers who share your interests. Getting a range of perspectives from diverse viewpoints will inform your work.

Conferences are another vehicle for expanding your network and encouraging diversity of thought. Whether virtual or in-person, the academic conference provides an opportunity for you to participate in the academic community. Many academic conferences offer a student discount, or feature a submission option for student-authored papers. From local to global, you'll find opportunities to share your work and connect to other scholars in your discipline. Attending academic conferences will keep you informed on new findings and the latest research in the form of papers or poster sessions. Academic conferences exist on every topic imaginable and in all corners of the globe. For the undergraduate researcher, it can be a transformative experience to attend and participate.

Data Collection and Analysis: For Future Consideration

As outlined at the start of the chapter, the focus here has been on digital tools and techniques for discovery, organization, and collaboration. It is necessary to acknowledge that many more opportunities exist for integrating digital solutions for research. In the realm of data collection, particularly for survey research, instruments such as Qualtrics or Google Forms can be valuable for collecting information on the attitudes and beliefs of research subjects. Instruments for voice recording and documenting can support field research or interviews. Qualitative software can help you manage, sort, and explore large amounts of data. Quantitative software can help you interpret data, whether you are dealing with simple descriptive statistics or working on more complex analyses. Both qualitative and quantitative software can generate reports, charts, and graphics to help you enhance your research narrative. In all of these instances, you'll find how-to guides and support online. Some tools will have a steeper learning curve than others, but any progress you make in adopting and using a tool for research will enhance your overall ability to find and apply technological solutions for your academic endeavors.

If you are interested in gaining knowledge about a particular research tool, many opportunities exist for self-directed learning that can enhance what you are learning in your college classes. Massive Open Online Courses (MOOCs) like Coursera or EdX offer instruction in a range of topics that could benefit an undergraduate researcher. For example, you could take a short course on how to use SPSS software or how to create a survey. Most MOOCs are free, although you can pay to earn a formal credential. Other online sources may provide you with the instruction you need to elevate understanding of research tools, such as LinkedIn Learning (a subscription service that you may have access to through your college) or even YouTube. Be sure to apply the same critical lens to training sources that you use when evaluating a research source—consider the background and motivation of the creator, confirm the timeliness of the content, evaluate the intended audience, and cross-check with other sources of information (Purdue Writing Lab, n.d.). The time you take to learn a tool can make a huge difference in your ability to efficiently use it for research.

Presenting Your Work

When it comes time to present your research, consider your audience before anything else. If the audience is not familiar with your topic, be sure to define your terminology and provide context for why your research is important. At most academic talks, time constraints require you to distill an in-depth research project down to the most salient points, so keep that in mind when building your presentation. For live presentations where you will create slides or a poster to communicate this information, use your materials to tell a story (Tips for Presenting Your Research Effectively, 2014). Avoid cramming too much text onto a slide or a poster. Images and charts can be an effective way to support your talk and provide a visual for your spoken words. Giving an asynchronous presentation with voiceover? Be sure to provide closed captions for accessibility.

For slide decks, cloud options like Google Slides or Prezi offer the benefit of storage as well as portability. In the event that you need to share your slides with your audience after the presentation is over, you can control the access and distribute your slide deck as you see fit (to specific people or publicly—or as a PDF). PowerPoint or Keynote are also options, but be prepared for font changes if you are presenting on a computer that is not the one used for creating the presentation. Regardless of what tool you choose, consider font size and color choices that improve readability and utilize best practices in universal design. Add alt-text to any images you use in order to make your shared presentation accessible with a screen reader. If you distribute a PDF or Word Document version of your paper, use headings and document styles to improve navigation.

Conclusion

Your undergraduate education may be the last academic degree you pursue, or you may continue to a graduate program. Undergraduate research, coupled with an appreciation for technology's role in strengthening and enhancing your work, can have a lifelong benefit. Research can influence public policy, inspire change, and educate. It can help you prepare to advocate for the things that matter to you in your community. Even now, your contributions as a student-scholar can have an impact on your campus, in your field, and in the community. The problem-solving and search strategies you cultivate will help you any time you need to access information and make sense of findings. Your relationship with research mentors and the networking you do with other scholars will strengthen your student experience and prepare you for other types of collaborative work. Your enhanced critical thinking skills will influence how you interpret research findings in everyday life.

And yet, not all digital research tools age well. What is a popular option now may be obsolete in ten years. For this reason, it is critical to embrace the concepts you learn through the *application* of digital solutions and not limit yourself to specific products. Embrace the spirit of digital literacy and apply your critical thinking skills to help you make good decisions in your discovery—regardless of the tools you use to search. Engage reference librarians to get your research plan off to a strong start. Maintain a consistent habit of digital organization. Find a mentor to guide you through the process and perhaps even collaborate with you on projects. Look around for other scholars who share your research interests and support each other in your pursuit of excellence in your work. Get comfortable using as many tools as you have available, and if you need to invest time in learning how to use a tool, take the time to explore the features and get the most out of your time investment. As you integrate digital tools and create research deliverables for sharing, give thought to making your documents accessible.

Expanding your comfort with a range of digital solutions will allow you to be ready for evolving technologies that benefit your research as well as other professional and personal pursuits. If the tool you are comfortable with is someday no longer available or is replaced, you'll be able to shift gears and progress onward. With a sound foundation underlying your approach to research, you can make the most of the digital tools you use to support your research goals now and for the future.

References

About Google Scholar. (n.d.). Retrieved from https://scholar.google.com/intl/en/scholar/about.html

Connaway, L. S., Dickey, T. J., & Radford, M. L. (2011). "If it is too inconvenient I'm not going after it:" Convenience as a critical factor in information-seeking behaviors. *Library & Information Science Research, 33*(3), 179–190. doi:10.1016/j.lisr.2010.12.002

Council on Undergraduate Research. (n.d.). Retrieved from https://www.cur.org/who/organization/mission_and_vision/

Hargittai, E., & Walejko, G. (2008). The participation divide: Content creation and sharing in the digital age1. *Information, Communication & Society, 11*(2), 239–256. doi:10.1080/13691180801946150

Kirkwood, P. (2011). Shaping the curriculum: The power of a library's digital resources. *Computers in Libraries, 31*(4), 6–11.

Losh, E. (2021). Universities must stop assuming that all students are tech-savvy. *Times Higher Education.* https://www.timeshighereducation.com/opinion/universities-must-stop-presuming-all-students-are-tech-savvy

Miller, S., & Murillo, N. (2012). Why don't students ask librarians for help?: Undergraduate help-seeking behavior in three academic libraries, in *College Libraries and Student Culture: What We Now Know*, edited by Lynda M. Duke & Andrew D. Asher, 53–55 (Chicago, IL: American Library Association, 2011).

Perruso, C. (2016). Undergraduates' use of Google vs. library resources: A four-year cohort study. *College & Research Libraries, 77*(5), 614–630. doi:10.5860/crl.77.5.614

Purdue Writing Lab. (n.d.). General Guidelines // Purdue Writing Lab. Retrieved from https://owl.purdue.edu/owl/research_and_citation/conducting_research/evaluating_sources_of_information/general_guidelines.html#:~:text=Evaluating Sources: General Guidelines 1 Find Out What,... 9 Examine the List of References.

Springshare. (n.d.). The SaaS Platform for Libraries and Educational Institutions. Retrieved from https://springshare.com/

Tips for Presenting Your Research Effectively. (2014). American Psychological Association. Retrieved from https://www.apa.org/science/about/psa/2014/02/presenting

Todorinova, L. (2015). Wikipedia and undergraduate research trajectories. *New Library World, 116*(3/4), 201–212. doi:10.1108/nlw-07-2014-0086Vaidhyanathan, S. (2008). Generational myth. *The Chronicle of Higher Education, 55*(4), B.7.

Vinyard, M., Mullally, C., & Colvin, J. B. (2017). Why do students seek help in an age of DIY? Using a qualitative approach to look beyond statistics. *Reference & User Services Quarterly, 56*(4), 257. doi:10.5860/rusq.56.4.257

Vondracek, R. (2007). Comfort and convenience? Why students choose alternatives to the library. *Portal: Libraries and the Academy, 7*(3), 277–293. doi:10.1353/pla.2007.0039

6 Building Essential Components of a Research Project

Determining Topic, Research Design, and Ethical Conduct Need

Giang-Nguyen T. Nguyen and Carla J. Thompson

In recent years, multiple authors have emphasized the need for including undergraduate research in programs for preparing teachers (Linn et al., 2015; Lopatto, 2004, 2010). Undergraduate students may misinterpret the expression "conducting research" as locating information in a library or through online resources; however, that process is more appropriately known as conducting a literature review or reviewing current literature (McGowan, 2021). Exploring the process of research includes (a) learning new terminology, (b) understanding the potential risks to human participants, (c) data analysis, (d) interpretation of results, and (e) disseminating research findings.

Although the benefits of undergraduate research experiences are well known, students still face many challenges when beginning research. Students often lack the support they need to ensure success during the research process (Balster, Pfund, Rediske, & Branchaw, 2010). Brown (2006) noted that challenges may be especially overwhelming for those from nonacademic backgrounds and for underrepresented minority students, who may feel isolated or intimidated by the behavioral norms of the research environment. Perhaps the most challenging components facing undergraduate students in conducting research is narrowing down the research topic, selecting an appropriate research design, and understanding the importance of research ethics and the ethical roles of researchers involved in conducting research.

In the previous chapters, you were introduced to reading academic articles, exploring academic writing, and conducting a review of pertinent literature. Conducting a literature review enables researchers to find the "gap" in the literature and reveals which topics are remaining and needing to be explored for completing an exhaustive literature review. A gap in the literature could be considered a problem, something that may spur one's interest to delve into doing more research into literature pertinent to the topic. A researcher may also transform the gap in research into a well-defined problem by narrowing down the topic. This chapter provides an overview of the procedures and considerations for undergraduates to

DOI: 10.4324/9781003226475-6

conduct research in education, including (1) narrowing a research topic, (2) selecting an appropriate research design, and (3) understanding and practicing research ethics and working with the Institutional Review Board (IRB). In addition, this chapter guides students through the practice of complex iterative and transferable skills that lead to efficient, methodical, and ethical conduct of the basic steps in the research process. At the end of this chapter, you will have traversed the multiple procedures involved in conducting research.

Narrowing Down the Topic

This chapter demonstrates and encourages the use of participatory skills, for example, negotiating a topic choice with a faculty member/instructor and/or the practice of employing patient and persistent navigation for choosing and validating a feasible topic for engaging in research. In conducting a literature review, individuals may find many topics of interest; however, every researcher must learn how to narrow down a topic for investigation. The process may be seen as a negotiation process utilizing high cognitive demands. Each individual researcher has to consider several different factors involved in conducting research, such as time, resources, access to research sites, decisions about how to collect information or data, analysis and processing of gathered data/information to develop conclusions, and ways to present and disseminate research findings. Particularly, if the topic is too broad, the researcher may find it difficult to complete the research in a timely manner.

This process of formulating a research question is described in the sequence demonstrated in Figure 6.1: (1) choose a general research topic or idea, (2) identify the purpose or problem statement for conducting the research, and (3) formulate a research question. Figure 1 depicts how a researcher can zoom outward from creating an idea for researching, to generating a problem statement to explore, and then simplifying the

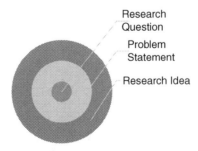

Figure 6.1 The process of formulating research questions.

problem statement into a research question. This triad process is especially useful for education students just beginning to grasp the process of formulating a research question for investigation, that is, begin with a researchable idea, develop a problem statement, and then generate a research question.

Action Research

Action research is often used to demonstrate how researchers narrow down a topic for conducting research. This type of research is commonly used in teacher education, especially involving researching classroom practices; it also allows researchers the flexibility of involving themselves within the research process to help improve their own practices. According to Mills (2014), action research is conducted by teachers, administrators, counselors, and others with interest in the teaching and learning process. Action research involving undergraduate students who are preparing to be classroom teachers include the following examples: (a) desiring to learn about the impact or effect of a certain teaching approach or method on student achievement, (b) determining how specific types of teaching methods may impact student learning, (c) determining how students learn, and (d) discerning how to improve teaching and learning practices (Metler, 2019). In addition, teacher participation in the development of educational research questions indicate teachers are aware of the problems in the classroom, and, by initiating actions regarding these problems, teachers become catalysts for change.

Teachers also serve as responsible agents for the improvement of their own classroom teaching, thereby utilizing research findings for uplifting teaching and learning (Ulla, Barrera, & Acompanado, 2017). Therefore, teachers conduct classroom research to fully understand the problems in the classroom and how those problems can be addressed in order to improve the teaching and learning process. Specifically, conducting/doing action research enables teachers to discover what went wrong, what went right, and what could be done to address multiple types of issues in the classroom (Ulla et al., 2017).

Narrowing the Topic by Negotiation with the Mentor

Undergraduate students conducting research will work on a research project with the guidance of a mentor, usually a faculty member, instructor, or administrator. Students may work on faculty-or student-initiated research projects (Beckman & Hensel, 2009). The project may involve one student or multiple students working together. And the students may be mentored by one faculty member or several working together to resolve an educational concern or investigate a question.

The following scenario provides an example of how one student worked with one faculty mentor on a student-initiated project. First, the student-researcher had to decide on and narrow down a research topic.

> Wendy is a junior in the teacher education program. She has been doing her field experience in the local school district. She noticed that various technologies are being used in the classrooms. Some she found very interesting and wished that she had been able to use them when she was a K-12 student. However, she also finds that some technologies were not very helpful. Through her own research, she learned that the school district has contributed a great amount of money to provide professional development and resources on the use of technology in teaching, which in turn may improve student learning. Therefore, Wendy would like to learn more about the use of technology in the classroom and to determine whether the use of technology in the classroom has any impact on student achievement.

In the example, one can see that Wendy's research interest is in the area of classroom technology and its impact on student achievement. The topic sounds interesting to Wendy, but she has a big task ahead of her. She needs to narrow down a very broad topic area. So Wendy has scheduled a meeting with a mentor in which she will share her interest but also negotiate with her mentor to narrow the scope of the research she plans to carry out.

When Wendy meets with her faculty mentor, Dr. Mark, they discuss questions she has about the general topic of classroom technology and student achievement. Dr. Mark understands the importance of encouraging students to develop a passionate interest in a particular topic and then to design their own research projects, with the guidance of a faculty mentor. Because the primary purpose of undergraduate research is to foster student learning (Beckman & Hensel, 2009), the emphasis for Dr. Mark is on helping Wendy move along a developmental trajectory in the practice of research. The developmental process might begin in the first year of college and continue until the student is capable of doing more independent research (Beckman & Hensel, 2009). At the meeting, Wendy and Dr. Mark discuss some questions to help Wendy narrow down the topic:

- What do I mean by *technology*, specifically? Which educational technologies (e.g., software, applications, websites, hardware, equipment) am I referring to?
- Do I mean the use of technology as general tools (e.g., smart boards) or content-specific software or applications (e.g., software to teach reading or arithmetic)?
- Which grade levels do I want to look at? Which student groups within those grades?

- What problems do I see in integrating technology into teaching and learning?
- Which academic disciplines/subject areas do I want to study?

After a long discussion and thinking about these questions, Wendy decided to focus on mathematics at the middle-school level. Those steps led Wendy to formulate a purpose for her research: *The purpose of this study will be to examine the effect of using technology on student motivation for learning mathematics.* After some further exploration about technological tools used in middle-school mathematics, she identified some possibilities: Geometer's Sketchpad, Desmos, TI-graphing calculators, and GeoGebra. Wendy realized she was most intrigued by GeoGebra, an interactive, general mathematics app that can be used by students at various levels.

The research question she decided to examine is, **How does the use of GeoGebra technology influence the motivation of middle-school students enrolled in Algebra I?** After formulating a research question, Wendy started looking for an appropriate research design.

Selecting an Appropriate Research Design

This section **helps students evaluate** their level of knowledge and uncover ways to strengthen and augment their capacities; for example, as in **the selection of an appropriate research design, which requires knowledge of designs** and how to align a research design with the topic and research question(s). The research question drives the research design. Research design is an individual plan to carry out the appropriate tasks for addressing or answering the research question. Research designs include qualitative methods, quantitative methods, or mixed methods (a combination of qualitative and quantitative methods).

Qualitative Research Design

Qualitative research is a process of collecting and analyzing data that are non-numerical (Creswell & Poth, 2018). In education, qualitative research methods heavily depend on the following types of data: classroom observations, focus-group discussions, in-depth interviews, texts/documents, and other non-numerical information.

In the example, in which Wendy decided to conduct her research in an Algebra I class at a local middle school, she could choose qualitative research methods. Her qualitative data sources might include (a) classroom observations whereby Wendy takes notes in her researcher's memo book, (b) teacher briefs or short-answer responses from the teacher to a set of qualitative questions, (c) a student questionnaire provided for students to write in short answers, and (d) student interviews conducted by a trained interviewer or Wendy. The student data (c and d) would be students' responses to questions about their views of the technology (GeoGebra) that their teacher has been using in the course.

Quantitative Research Design

Quantitative research depends on numeric values. In analyzing quantitative data, a researcher must have a background in mathematics and statistics to perform the data analyses and to interpret the results (Creswell, 2014); student-researchers without that background may have a faculty mentor who can conduct the analyses. Quantitative data sources include questionnaires and surveys with designated responses, such as a Likert scale, typically a 5- or 7-point scale of agreement. A 5-point Likert scale, for example, might designate 1 for "strongly disagree," 2 for "disagree," 3 for "neither agree nor disagree," 4 for "agree," and 5 for "strongly agree." For high-quality research studies, the survey instrument should be validated and reliable (Creswell, 2014) and created by an experienced survey researcher.

If Wendy wanted to use quantitative methods to investigate the influence of technology on student motivation in the Algebra I course, she might utilize validated, reliable instruments for measuring motivation, such as the Intrinsic Motivation Inventory and the Instructional Materials Motivation Survey (Loorbach, Peters, Karreman, & Steehouder, 2015). The Intrinsic Motivation Survey is obtained free for research use from the site www. selfdetermination.org. It has been empirically tested in multiple classroom settings, so it has been validated and determined to be reliable. Sometimes researchers have to purchase a survey or other type of instrument to use. Other times, researchers need to develop an original survey or other type of data-gathering tool, also known as an instrument, for data collection. When a researcher develops an original instrument, they usually perform pilot testing of the instrument with a group before using it for a formal research study. Such piloting helps determine the instrument's reliability and validity.

As Figure 6.2 illustrates, both qualitative and quantitative data provide evidence in research studies. Neither one is better than the other. Each method should be selected based on the needs of the researcher and the study.

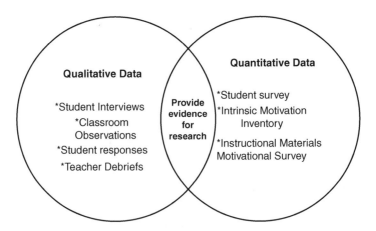

Figure 6.2 Data sources for each research design.

Mixed-Methods Research Design: Combining Qualitative and Quantitative Data

A mixed-methods research design combines qualitative and quantitative types of data. Wendy identified both qualitative and quantitative data sources, and she could decide to use both. For example, Wendy could use a questionnaire with Likert-scale responses (e.g., 1–5 scale with 1 indicating "strongly disagree" and 5 indicating "strongly agree") to get quantitative data about the students' opinions. The responses would then be calculated to produce a numerical score. Wendy could also use a survey with "open response" questions that ask respondents to write sentences or even paragraphs about their opinions and experiences. Those written responses would be considered qualitative data. Using both types of instruments—a Likert-scale questionnaire and an open-response survey—would constitute a mixed-methods research design.

In a mixed-methods research study, researchers analyze the qualitative and quantitative data to determine how they align or come together or whether they indicate interesting differences. A mixed-methods research design usually generates more data for the researcher to analyze as compared to using either qualitative or quantitative methods alone. Therefore, using mixed methods may require more time for the researcher to collect and analyze the data.

In order to determine whether she would choose a qualitative, quantitative, or mixed-methods research design, Wendy considered the following questions:

• When can the data collection begin? At what point does it need to be completed?
• Which types of data will be feasible to collect?
• What items/questions do I want to ask students?
• What data analysis tools will be used to analyze the data?
• Where and how will interviews take place, if interviews are conducted?
• How will I be able to obtain child assent (agreement from research participants under the age of 18) and permission from their parents/guardians (required for research involving minors)?

The research question Wendy proposed and the timeline that she had available for collecting and analyzing her data caused her to decide to conduct a quantitative study. Her timeline follows in Table 6.1.

Table 6.2 provides examples of research questions and data sources that could be used to address the posited research questions.

Choosing a research design and determining the data collection procedures involve planning and skill. Researchers also need to consider ethical issues involved in conducting research. The next section will discuss ethics in research and provide students some of the necessary preparations and considerations prior to beginning a research project.

Table 6.1 Data Collection Timeline

Research Activities	08/21	09/21	10/21-/21	12/21	1/22–3/22
School visit	*Visit institution site *Get contact information *Discuss the schedule with the teacher				
Consent forms (child assent) (parent consent)		*Send consent home to parents *Hold a Q&A session for parents			
Data collection analysis (continuous data analysis)			*Student survey	*Triangulation *Process mapping outcomes *Convergent quantitative and qualitative data	
Writing up report					Write up results

Table 6.2 Research Questions and Data Sources

Research Question	Research Design	Data Source
What are students' expressed experiences in an Algebra 1 course?	Qualitative	Classroom observations Student interviews Students questionnaires
How did students' interest levels in the course change throughout the semester within an Algebra 1 course?	Quantitative	Course interest survey
In what ways does a teacher influence student motivation within an Algebra I course?	Mixed methods	Course instructional materials Motivational survey Student interview Classroom observations

Before Wendy will be able to conduct her research study, she must complete some important actions required of all researchers working with "human subjects" (or "human participants") prior to beginning the research. These activities include (a) participating in training, and obtaining a certificate of completion, for the protection of human subjects and (b) submitting an application to the college or university's IRB to request permission to conduct research involving human subjects/participants.

These activities are required of all researchers who intend to gather data from and about humans in a research study. The training for researchers has to be periodically updated every three to five years, depending on the nature of the research; however, the researcher must complete an application to the IRB for every study that involves human subjects/participants. The research cannot begin until the IRB approves it. The purpose of this process is for researchers to guarantee they are not violating the rights of the individuals (humans) involved in the research project. The IRB committee at every college and university (as well as all research hospitals, school districts, and other places where research on human subjects/participants is conducted) operates for the protection of those individuals. This step in the research process is a critical component of all research involving humans. Researchers conducting research with humans must demonstrate cognizance of the various ethical considerations associated with such research. The next section focuses on researchers' multiple ethical considerations.

Ethical Issues in Conducting Research

This section of the chapter leads students through the **multiple ethical concerns** related to conducting research, especially regarding the use of human subjects and harmful materials. Emphasis is placed on adherence to rigorous ethical considerations governed within each college's or university's IRB. In addition to having the IRB's approval, researchers working within schools need the permission of school and district administrators.

> Wendy hopes to conduct her research study at a local middle school. Wendy knows a mathematics teacher, Ms. Watkins, at the middle school where she previously did her field experience, so she contacted Ms. Watkins and met with her. After Ms. Watkins agreed to use her class for the study, they both met with the principal. Fortunately, the principal was very supportive of Wendy's research because it aligns with one of the school's initiatives regarding classroom technology. Even though both the teacher and the principal support Wendy's research, the principal indicated that Wendy must also get approval from the district superintendent's office before she can collect any data. That permission is required before Wendy and her faculty mentor can even apply for IRB approval.

Conducting educational research involves all types of people: parents, students, school leaders, teachers, politicians, children, and people with disabilities—many of whom have little or no knowledge of research or their rights to participate or refuse to participate in research. Multiple ethical concerns are related to involving people in the process of conducting research. Human beings are vulnerable to potential risks by participating in research projects.

A national governing body in the United States, the Office of Research Integrity (ORI), is responsible for overseeing the ethical operations of all researchers who involve humans as subjects for research purposes. The ORI is a key office within the U.S. Department of Health and Human Services (HHS): https://ori.hhs.gov. The ORI is the responsible national agency for research issues in education and related fields involving the need for the protection of humans engaged in research as investigators and/or human subjects or participants in research projects. The ORI provides strict rules and protocols for protecting research participants and researchers, while assisting with the encouragement and guidelines for conducting responsible research. Understanding and abiding by strict rules and policies governing universal principles of ethical research are paramount considerations of all researchers prior to conducting any type of human-participants research, survey, or data-gathering activity. Researchers need to be familiar with the local governing body within their respective institution to get approval for conducting research. This local, institution-based body also involved in examining and approving research projects within the university is known as the Institutional Review Board (IRB). The IRB is charged with examining the risk of potential harm to human beings.

As an undergraduate student, you might have had some prior exposure to ethics and ethical procedures within your coursework, as you have been preparing to enter the world of teaching and/or school administration. However, the need to become fully prepared in the language and operational conditions aligned with conducting educational research must include a full unit of study/preparation devoted to the ethical considerations and responsibilities associated with conducting research. One area nationally approved by the ORI includes the listing of the nine principles of Responsible Conduct of Research (RCR) and applies to all levels and types of research involving human subjects. Undergraduate education majors should be aware of the nine principles, especially pertinent to classroom ethics and research associated with minors. They involve (1) Data Acquisition, Management, Sharing, and Ownership; (2) Conflict of Interest and Commitment; (3) Human Subjects Protection; (4) Animal Welfare; (5) Research Misconduct; (6) Publication Practices and Responsible Authorship; (7) Mentor/Trainee Responsibilities; (8) Peer Review; and (9) Collaborative Science (ORI).

Student-researchers work closely with their faculty mentors to prepare IRB applications. The guidance of an experienced researcher is essential for helping students respond to the IRB questions and explain the research procedures. At some colleges and universities, undergraduate students can be listed as the principal investigator (PI) or lead researcher on the IRB application. Others require a faculty mentor to serve as PI, and students are listed as co-investigators or collaborators on the research team.

Each institution has different requirements, but the following components are commonly required to submit an IRB application:

1   An IRB application form. Student-researchers should consult with their mentor when completing the application form. The application form will likely require the student's as well as the faculty mentor's signature; typically, all researchers involved in the project must be listed on and must sign the form to indicate knowledge of the research protocol. The application usually includes questions about the recruitment of human participants, such as which population will be researched? How will the researchers get access to the participants?

2   Consent forms. These convey information about the study and agreement of the individuals involved to participate. Child assent (agreement from a minor to participate) and parent/guardian permission are needed for research involving anyone under 18 years of age (e.g., K–12 students). For adult research subjects/participants (e.g., teachers to be interviewed), their informed consent is required.

3   Questionnaires, surveys, and/or other instruments. If the instruments were created by other researchers, you may need to request permission from those researchers to use them.

4   Certificate of completion of ethics training. At most U.S. institutions, the CITI (Collaborative Institutional Training Initiative) certificate or its equivalent, for all researchers (PI and co-investigators), is required

as part of the IRB application. Most colleges and universities have subscriptions to the online CITI training for students and faculty to enroll at no cost to them.

5   Letter from the cooperating site, if applicable. In the case of the example, Wendy had to seek permission from the school district she was planning to work in for her study. Each school district has a different approval process.

It is important to understand that the requirements are not obstacles to prevent you from conducting the research; they are safeguards for the people participating. The IRB approval indicates that planned research has minimal risk and is ethical.

Summary, Conclusion, and Implications

Conducting research is rewarding. Atay (2006) reported that

> studies have shown that teacher research has a profound effect on those who have done it, in some cases transforming classrooms and schools. It has been found to facilitate teachers' critical thought, boost teachers' self-esteem, and increase their awareness of students' needs.
>
> (p. 1)

Generally, research has a lot of benefits for in-service teachers in their professional development (Hine, 2013). According to Hine (2013), research equips teachers and other education practitioners with the skills necessary for identifying problems in a school and knowing how to address problems systematically. Research also serves as an opportunity for educators to self-evaluate their teaching practices (Hong & Lawrence, 2011). As a result, teachers can make changes in their pedagogical practices that aim to have a positive impact on teaching and learning (Mahani & Molki, 2012). Furthermore, research is a great form of improving teachers' lifelong learning and of continuing professional development (Ulla et al., 2017).

References

Atay, D. (2006). Teachers' professional development: Partnerships in research. *Tesl-Ej, 10*(2), 1–15.

Balster, N., Pfund, C., Rediske, R., & Branchaw, J. (2010). Entering research: A course that creates community and structure for beginning undergraduate researchers in the STEM disciplines. *CBE—Life Sciences Education, 9*(2), 108–118. https://doi.org/10.1187/cbe.09-10-0073

Beckman, M., & Hensel, N. (2009). Making explicit the implicit: Defining undergraduate research. *CUR Quarterly, 29*(4), 40–44.

Brown, B. A. (2006). "It isn't no slang that can be said about this stuff": Language, identity, and appropriating science discourse. *Journal of Research in Science Teaching, 43*(1), 96–126. https://doi.org/10.1002/tea.20096

Creswell, J. W. (2014). *Research design: Qualitative, quantitative, and mixed methods approaches* (4th ed.). Thousand Oaks, CA: Sage Publishers.

Creswell, J. W., & Poth, C. N. (2018). *Qualitative inquiry research design.* Thousand Oaks, CA: Sage Publishers.

Hine, G. S. C. (2013). The importance of action research in teacher education programs. *Issues in Educational Research, 23*(2): Special Issue, 151–163. http://www.iier.org.au/iier23/hine.pdf

Hong, C. E., & Lawrence, S. A. (2011). Action research in teacher education: Classroom inquiry, reflection, and data-driven decision making. *Journal of Inquiry and Action in Education, 4*(2), 1–17. http://www.wpunj.edu/dotAsset/330733.pdf

Linn, M. C., Palmer, E., Baranger, A., Gerard, E., & Stone, E. (2015). Undergraduate research experiences: Impacts and opportunities. *Science, 347*(6222), 1261757. https://doi.org/10.1126/science.1261757

Loorbach, N., Peters, O., Karreman, J., & Steehouder, M. (2015). Validation of the Instructional Materials Motivation Survey (IMMS) in a self-directed instructional setting aimed at working with technology. *British Journal of Educational Technology, 46*(1), 204–218.

Lopatto, D. (2004). Survey of undergraduate research experiences (SURE): First findings. *Cell Biology Education, 3*(4), 270–277. https://doi.org/10.1187/cbe.04-07-0045

Lopatto, D. (2010). Undergraduate research as a high-impact student experience. *Peer Review, 12*(2), 27–30.

Mahani, S., & Molki, A. (2012). Enhancing the quality of teaching and learning through action research. *Journal of College Teaching & Learning, 9*(3), 209–216. https://doi.org/10.19030/tlc.v9i3.7086

McGowan, B. (2021, February 26). *Literature review. Conducting & writing.* University of West Florida. https://libguides.uwf.edu/litreview

Metler, C. (2019). *Action research improving schools and empowering educators.* Thousand Oaks, CA: Sage Publications Inc.

Mills, G. E. (2014). *Action research: A guide for the teacher researcher* (5th ed.). London: Pearson. Office of Research Integrity (ORI). (n.d.). https://ori.hhs.gov

Ulla, M. B., Barrera, K. I. B., & Acompanado, M. M. (2017). Philippine classroom teachers as researchers: Teachers' perceptions, motivations, and challenges. *Australian Journal of Teacher Education, 42*(11), 52–64. https://doi.org/10.14221/ajte.2017v42n11.4

7 Data Analysis

The Heart of the Research Study

Deborah L. Thompson

Research handbooks, depending on the authorial source, feature outlines of five to ten essential steps in the research process. Each set of steps is comparable: (a) Identify the research problem, (b) Formulate the research question(s), (c) Complete the literature review, (d) Select appropriate methodology, (e) Collect data, (f) Analyze data. It is this last step that is the focus of this chapter. Data analysis is the process of systematically applying statistical and/or logical techniques to describe and illustrate, condense and recap, and evaluate **data**. Simply put, data analysis is a data reveal, that is, what the collected data tell the researcher. When analyzed appropriately, the data provide the answers to the research questions, inform conclusions, and support further decision-making and new or different ways to research a problem. This chapter guides students carefully through the analysis process, to ensure understanding of the steps involved in discovering the stories research data have to tell.

Qualitative Data, Quantitative Data, or Mixed-Methods Research

Data analyses must complement the type of data collected. Qualitative data are textual. They are non-numerical. They can be in the form of videos, audio recordings, journals, field notes, and photographs. Bogdan and Biklen (1998) describe qualitative data as

> rich in descriptions of people, places, and conversations, and not easily handled by statistical procedures. Research questions are not framed by operationalizing variables; rather, they are formulated to investigate topics in all their complexity, in context. While people conducting qualitative research may develop a focus as they collect data, they do not approach the research with specific questions to answer or hypotheses to test.
>
> (p. 2)

Among the methods of collecting qualitative data are *ethnography*, the *case study narrative inquiry, phenomenology*, and *grounded theory*. See Figure 7.1 for brief definitions of terms.

DOI: 10.4324/9781003226475-7

A Brief Definition of Research Terms

QUALITATIVE

Case study—An in-depth investigation of a single individual, family, event, or other entity (*APA Dictionary of Psychology* (https://dictionary.apa.org/case-studies)

Ethnography—A study of participants in a particular social or cultural setting, e.g., Papua New Guinea, a classroom or a church

Grounded theory—A method in which the study's theories are "grounded in the data" and are developed post data collection instead of pre-data collection (Glaser & Straus, 1967)

Narrative inquiry—A method in which storytelling is used to mode of understanding social patterns.

Phenomenology—A method that focuses on a subject's lived experiences.

QUANTITATIVE

Correlational—Research designed to establish a relationship between two closely-related entities and how one impacts the other, for example, what is the correlation between sleep apnea and high blood pressure?

Descriptive—Research designed to describe a situation, a population or a phenomenon. Descriptive research can explain the who, what, where and how, but not the why.

Experimental—A research design that adheres to a scientific research design. Includes a hypothesis, randomization of subjects to groups, a variable or variables that can be manipulated by the researcher, and variables that can be measured, calculated and compared.

Quasi-experimental—A research design that involves testing hypotheses but in which subjects are not randomly assigned to groups.

Measures of Central Tendency help the researcher find the middle or average of a data set.

- *Mode* is the most frequent value. For example, in this numerical array: 2, 5, 4, 6, 7, 5, 5, 8, the most frequent value is 5.
- *Median* is the value in the middle of the data.
  - Median of an odd numbered array: 1-2-9-7-5. Place values in numerical order: 1, 2, 5,7,9. To calculate the median is n+1/2. N=5+1=6/2=3. The median of the odd number array is in the # 3 position-5. Even number array: 1,2,3,9,7,5. Arrange in numerical order: 1, 2, 3, 5, 7, 9. N/2 and N/2+1; N/2=3 and N=6/2+1=4. The median values are in positions 3 and 4: 3 and 5
- *Mean or arithmetic mean* is the average of all values. The mean of the following array: 12+13+15=30(sum)/3(number of values) is 10.

Validity—Data or findings that are accurate, factual, true, correct.

Reliability—Data that are dependable, consistent. Reliable experiments produce the same results on repeated trials.

Variability—Describes the spread between data points from each other and from the center of a distribution. The measure of variability is the standard deviation (SD). **A hypothetical:** Say for example, the bane of high school juniors and seniors—the College Board's SATs—has a mean of 500 and a standard deviation of 100. That would translate to a score range (or spread) of 400-600—which according to the College Board is where the bulk of all SAT takers would fall.

Generalizability—Describes the extent to which findings of a study of one group or phenomenon can be successfully applied to another group or phenomenon that has not been studied.

Figure 7.1 A brief definition of research terms.

Each method is composed of data that have been collected in real time and in a natural context where people are interacting with one another and the researcher, for example, a classroom, playground, neighborhood, church, barbershop/beauty salon, or street corner. Common tools of qualitative data collection are interviews, open-response survey questions, observations, stories, case studies, and documents.

Quantitative data are quantifiable, that is, the information can be counted and converted to numbers to which statistical analyses are applied. Quantitative data can be generated from multiple-choice questions on surveys/questionnaires, experimental/quasi-experimental studies, and descriptive and correlational studies. The vocabulary of quantitative methods includes *large data sets* (which refer to sets of thousands or even millions of pieces of information: too many to process in a typical spreadsheet), *hypotheses*, *validity*, *reliability*, *variable*, and *generalizability*.

Albers (2017) considers quantitative data analysis as not "numbers crunching" but a way to think critically about how to analyze the data. Although it is sometimes assumed that quantitative methods are the bailiwick of the natural sciences and qualitative methods of the social sciences, the truth is that both methods can be applied to research across disciplines. The determining factor is the type of methodology; thus, the type of analysis depends on what the researcher wants to discover and the purpose of the study. Once the method is selected and the data are gathered, the appropriate analysis must be applied.

Data from mixed-methods research (MMR) are a combination of qualitative and quantitative data. Johnson (2007), cited in Schoonenboom and Johnson (2017), defines mixed-methods research as

> the type of research in which a researcher or team of researchers combines elements of qualitative and quantitative research approaches (e.g., use of qualitative and quantitative viewpoints, data collection\ analysis, inference techniques) for the broad purposes of breadth and depth of understanding and corroboration.
>
> (p. 108)

An example of mixed-methods research (MMR). Mixed-methods research studies can be found across the disciplinary spectrum. I was a classroom teacher when I began my dissertation research in the late 1980s. The state of Tennessee had just implemented one of the first in the nation high-stakes testing programs. I[1] wanted to discover how high-stakes state testing[2] influenced literacy instruction in three different elementary school settings: urban, rural, and suburban. Quantitative data were collected from 200 elementary school teachers and administrators across the three school settings using a semantic differential scale. A semantic differential scale measured teachers' beliefs about testing based on paired antonyms such as helpful/unhelpful, good/bad, warranted/unwarranted, valid/invalid. Quantitative data were analyzed using simple statistics: T tests and analysis of variance (ANOVA). Qualitative data were collected from interviews from a subsample of the 200 teachers and administrators (purposively sampled)[3] who had completed the semantic differential scale. These interviews were transcribed, and the transcripts were analyzed using a cross-site analysis (Miles & Huberman, 1984). A cross-site analysis is used to compare themes, stories, subjects' word choices, and so on, across multiple sites—in this case, different school sites. (In addition to education, cross-site analysis is used in the health and environmental fields.)

Basic Steps in Analyzing Qualitative and Quantitative Data

A perusal of any text or handbook on analyzing data reveals that there are a given set of steps for analyzing qualitative data. They are (a) preparing and organizing the data such as transcripts or field notes; (b) identifying and neutralizing researcher bias. Neutralizing personal biases prevents the researcher from influencing consciously or unconsciously the data analysis to arrive at the findings she or he wants instead of allowing the data to influence the findings; (c) reading through the data to discover themes to be coded; (d) coding the data; (e) searching for patterns in the coding. This is an iterative process that may call for the researcher to regroup and recode more than once; (f) building and verifying theories; and (g) drawing conclusions.

Samuels (2020) has created a simple guide for analyzing quantitative data. For novice researchers, only a few are applicable:

1   Process your data and create a raw data spreadsheet. (This step, Samuels states, is often overlooked.) Raw data are the unanalyzed results of data collection. Use raw data to verify findings. Two undergraduate researchers in sophomore practicum want to find out how well a certain math technique has helped the students in their third-grade class. All of the math scores before and after instruction would constitute raw data. After all scores are entered on a spreadsheet such as Excel, the data can be analyzed based on the variables the researchers choose—demographics, recent scores on math tests, grades in math, etc.

2   Use descriptive analysis to get a "feel" for your data. Descriptive analysis includes measures of central tendency and measures of variability. Measures of central tendency include mean, median, and mode. Measures of variability (or spread) include standard deviation, variance, and skewness.

3   Write a narrative to go with the descriptive statistics.

The Child Study: A Petri Dish for Generating Quantitative and Qualitative Data

Many elementary and early childhood education students complete their teacher education courses of study without any exposure to research studies or opportunities to conduct research except in their child development courses. Child development courses are available from institutions worldwide, from the UK to South Africa to Germany (naturally, as Germany is the home of the first kindergartens). Embedded in each child development course is the child study. Preservice students visit classrooms as participant observers to observe and record the activities of children in their natural classroom settings. The standard assignment calls for each preservice student to observe children for a given time and then make a selection of one or two children to observe for the duration of the semester—usually for 35–40 hours. Using a list of child developmental domains—social development, cognitive development, language development, physical development, and gross motor development—the students take field notes on their kindergarten or first- or second-grade subjects going through their normal classroom routines, including lunch and recess. The culmination of these observations is the child case study—a combination of the student's field notes, the subject's demographic information, the teacher's observations of the subject, and classroom artifacts, such as a copy of a subject's creative story, a picture of an art project, or a copy of a math test paper. These case studies are usually bound in a ring binder, graded, and picked up by the student and often never seen again. Just some tweaks of this standard assignment will produce a world of data that teacher education students can immerse themselves in to learn how to conduct research and analyze the data evolving from that research.

Revising the Child Study Using the Language Development Domains

After a major curricular transformation in the early 2000s, many teacher education courses in my department were set up as block courses. My early literacy class was teamed with the child development class (part of the sophomore block—science methods and math methods were the other half of the sophomore block). With few exceptions, everyone took the two courses as corequisites. The literacy class filled the early-morning block; the child development course, the after-lunch block. To better coordinate the assignments, the child development professor and I taught different aspects of the child study. I taught the concept of participant observer, including how to take effective field notes and how to code them for the different domains, especially the language development domains. The language development domain gave me an avenue into integrating course-embedded research in the early literacy class. I revised what students had to do with the child observations relative to the language development domain.

The early literacy extension (excerpted from my early literacy syllabus). In addition to the language development domain field notes for the child study assignment*, you will add the following items:

1   Three additional sets of language and play observations/field notes—observe your subject's use of language in three different settings—one in class, one in the lunchroom (if talking is allowed; if not, snack time), and one outdoors during free play or recess.
2   Spelling assessment using the primary spelling list from *Words Their Way.*
3   A modified *Concepts about Print* or *Running Record* (both by Marie Clay)
       *Given the volume of data generated by this assignment, you may use either of your students, if you are observing two students.

Types of data generated by the literacy assignments. There were copious amounts of data generated by these extended literacy assignments. Notice that the literacy assignments comprised a mixed-methods research study. The spelling assessment generated quantitative data. Each child study subject took a developmental spelling test (Bear, Invernizzi, Templeton, & Johnston, 2012)—adjusted for the semester the child observations were conducted (fall or spring). The developmental spelling list consisted of 26 words with specific feature points (totaling 56 for the entire list). The subjects were asked to spell/write as many words as they could. Some subjects stopped at five (the minimum required), while others carried on through the entire list. The data generated by this assessment were quantitative. Each subject's spelling list was analyzed for specific features, for example, initial consonants, final or terminal consonants, and short-vowel and long-vowel patterns. These features were recorded on a coded spread sheet. The feature category in which the subjects scored the most points was the spelling level at which they placed, for example, late emergent, early letter name. See Figure 7.2 for a modified example of the coding sheet.

The language and play observations generated qualitative data. The subjects were observed in three different contexts. These observations were recorded as field notes. I gave an in-class workshop on how to code field notes using the college student's favorite writing instrument—the neon highlighter. I developed a field note coding guide based on M. A. K. Halliday's seven language functions (1975). See Figure 7.3 for the seven categories. Upon coding and categorization of the language field notes, the preservice teachers were able to discern which linguistic contexts produced the most creative utterances, the most one-word utterances, and so on.

	Spelling Stage						
	Emergent		Letter Name			Within Word	
	Late	Early	Middle	Late	Early	Middle	Late
	Features						
	Consonants		Short Vowels	Digraphs	Blends	Common Long Vowels	
	Initial	Final					
Fan	F	N	A				
Pet	P	T	E				
Dig	D	G	I				
Rob	R	B	O				
Hope	H	P				o-e	
Wait	W	T				ai	
Gum	G	M	U				
Sled			E		sl		
Stick			I		St		
Shine				Sh		i-e	

Figure 7.2 An edited example of the primary spelling inventory features guide (Bear et al., 2012).

Function	Definition	Example
Instrumental	Used to satisfy personal needs or to get things done	I want some juice.
Regulatory	Used to tell others what to do.	Bring me my juice.
Interactional	Used to get along or to make contact with others	Do you want some of my juice?
Personal	Used to express self	I don't like tomato juice.
Heuristic	Used to gain knowledge about the world	How do they make orange juice?
Imaginative	Used to pretend, make believe or tell stories	I want to be a juice orange!
Representational	Used to convey facts/information	It takes two oranges to make a ½ a cup of juice.

Figure 7.3 Seven language functions (Halliday, 1975).

Quantitative	Qualitative
Strengths	Strengths
Generalizability due to randomization	Specificity (no randomization)
Consistency	Open-ended
Anonymity	Cost effective
Data can be collected quickly	Allows for collaboration
Large sample sizes	Greater chances for creativity
Replicable	Data are contextualized
Limitations	Limitations
Little chance to follow-up answers, e.g., in a questionnaire	Not generalizable
Subject mismatch with general population due to selection bias	Time consuming
Veracity of subjects	Labor intensive
Costly	Patterns/trends may be difficult to discern
Validity	Reliability

Figure 7.4 Selected strengths and weaknesses of data generated by quantitative and qualitative methodologies.

The data generated from the *Concepts about Print* and the *Running Record* were quantitative. In *Concepts about Print*, the subjects read selected pieces of texts from picture books. The student observers asked their subjects to demonstrate whether they could distinguish between a lower-case b and a lower-case d, the word *saw* from *was* or *how* from *who*, and where to start reading on a page. *Running Records* produce a number of miscues made when a student is reading connected texts. Miscues include substituting one word for another, omitting a word or phrase, and inserting words that are not present in the text. These quantifiable miscues produce a portrait of how well a student can read aloud. The literacy extensions not only produced quantitative and qualitative data, but they also were subject to the limitations of quantitative and qualitative data. See Figure 7.4 for strengths and limitations of quantitative and qualitative research and analysis.

A Classroom Examples of Coding Qualitative Data Using Content Analysis

Preservice teacher education courses provide a rich environment for embedded research projects. Typical assignments that include classroom observations make excellent platforms for introducing undergrads to elementary qualitative methodologies and data analyses. A typical classroom observation assignment can be converted to a simple discourse analysis assignment. Discourse analysis is a way to analyze spoken language in use tempered by the context in which the discourse occurs. There are several analytic tools of discourse data. For this assignment, students were taught to use a code and run a content analysis[4] on classroom language samples. (This assignment was a modification of the earlier literacy/child study assignment.)

Literacy. As with the earlier assignment, the observation units and coding schemes were based on M. A. K. Halliday's seven language functions. For in-class practice, the students were given a sample of field notes I composed as a participant observer in a small research study I had conducted. The objective of the research was to determine how book talk among students differed between a nonfiction picture book read aloud and a fiction picture book read aloud (not included in this sample). In small groups, my literacy students read the transcript and discussed how to analyze, code, and create categories for the read-aloud session. Truncated excerpts with the language functions labeled include the following:

CONTEXT: A small group nonfiction read-aloud session in a second-grade classroom during morning meeting. SUBJECTS: one teacher (female) and six students (3 females and 3 males)
TEXT: *The Magic School Bus at the Waterworks* (Cole, 1986)
THE INTRO TO MY FIELD NOTES: M (T in the transcript) is conducting an interactive read-aloud with *The Magic School Bus at the Waterworks* as part of Morning Workshop. M introduces the book with a series of questions to which the students respond. One of the students remarks that the classroom in the Magic School Bus book is a lot like their classroom:
F1: Teacher, instead of reading Miss Frizzle's name you can say your name, because you are like Miss Frizzle. **(regulatory/imaginative)**

M1: Yeah, and you can read some of the kids' names in this room instead of those in the book. **(imaginative)**

T: Yes, that would be fun.

M1: The kid with the glasses would be you Jason (pseudonym), and I can be one of the other boys in the book. **(imaginative)**

T: Let's get back to the book which is entitled *The Magic School Bus at the Waterworks.*

    She stops at important junctures so that students can respond to what has been read.

M2: I read that book before. It was a long time ago last year. I read it with you teacher, remember? The book is very funny. **(informational)**

F2 TO M2: How did you know about the book? Have you seen it before? **(heuristic)**

M2: She (the teacher) read it with me a long time ago. **(informational)**

T: Continues reading and asks students to respond to different pages in the book.

F2: Hey look, Miss Frizzle got on alligator shoes. And look at that dress. It's got alligators on it too! I wonder why she dresses like that. **(heuristic)**

T: This book will tell us how our city gets its clean water down to the last drop. As she finishes Water Fact #3, she asks: How many of you knew that?

F3 & M2: Knew what?

T: That water evaporates.

M1 AND F3: Remember we did that experiment with the bowl and the ice? And when we had steam coming from a pot just like a cloud? **(informational)**

T: Yes, we were discussing condensation. Who remembers what condensation means?

M2: Like when people talk to each other. **(informational)**

T: That's a good guess, because it does sound somewhat like the word, conversation, but they are not the same.

F2: It means like when it rains in the sky. Like on a glass with cold water and ice. **(informational)**

T: Great F2. I remember that you really liked that experiment.

Using the Halliday categories, pairs of students coded the entire transcript (like the short piece above). Then they consulted peers to clarify their findings relative to themes and categories. They tallied the responses of the students—girls or boys—and then created visuals to show who spoke more, used what functions more, and in what context. Who asked or used more representational language? Did all of the language functions fall in the second category considered the learning or heuristic functions? Were there examples of the doing functions, and if so, which doing function was used most frequently. Were there functions that could have fallen under more than one category? These types of activities provided undergraduates with many opportunities to learn how to analyze and write about data in their classes that they prepare them for the future. In working with simple data sets, preservice teachers acquire the skills to live and teach in a society where almost every aspect of education is or will be driven by big data.

Bias—A Major Limitation of Qualitative and Quantitative Research and Analysis

There are numerous weaknesses underlying quantitative and qualitative research. Perhaps the biggest weakness is that of bias. Bias is everywhere in research despite all good intentions to eradicate it. Although quantitative research has the reputation for being more objective, Haardörfer (2019) contends that decision-making in quantitative research is not as objective as has been touted. Subjective elements intervene, before any objective measures are employed, for example, what is climate change doing to the Alaskan bear population? Does the researcher study polar bears or Kodiack bears? The choice is subjective. Haardörfer states that by clinging to a veneer of objectivity, quantitative researchers have "impeded" advancement in some areas of research.

Researchers are often not aware how their personal biases interact and influence their research. For example, Silicon Valley tech companies have been having difficulties with their artificial intelligence (AI) algorithms.[5] Amazon discovered that their AI algorithms were biased against female hires and a health tech company discovered its AI algorithms were biased against minorities. (More on this type of bias later in the chapter.)

Sometimes these biases do not reveal themselves until a study has been completed, and the results highly praised. Perhaps one of the most famous examples of selection bias was Harvard University's Physicians' Health Study I, known colloquially as "the aspirin study."

Selection bias at the highest levels. Selection bias is related to the population from which the study sample is chosen (Pannucci & Wilkins, 2010). One of the most influential medical studies ever conducted was the Physicians' Health Study 1, and it is a prime example of selection bias. In 1981, researchers at Harvard Medical School and Brigham and Women's Hospital wanted to study the effects of aspirin on healthy male subjects. The study had two foci: to see if aspirin could prevent serious cardiovascular attacks and to see if beta-carotene prevented cancer. The researchers decided to recruit healthy **male** members from the membership rolls of the prestigious American Medical Association (AMA; https://phs.bwh.harvard.edu/phs1.htm#recruit). AMA at the time of the first study was overwhelmingly male and overwhelmingly white and skewed toward mid-aged men due to the expense of joining the organization. Selection bias was inevitable:

Consent forms and enrollment questionnaires were sent to all 261,248 male physicians between 40 and 84 years of age who lived in the

United States and who were registered with the American Medical Association. Almost half responded to the invitation. Of the 59,285 who were willing to participate in the trial, 26,062 were told they could not because they reported a history of myocardial infarction, stroke, or transient ischemic attack; cancer (except non-melanoma skin cancer); current renal or liver disease; peptic ulcer; gout; or contraindication to or current use of either aspirin or beta-carotene. The final sample consisted of 33,223 willing and eligible physicians.

(https://phs.bwh.harvard.edu/phs1.htm#recruit)

The trials had not been running long before outstanding results emerged. The results of the aspirin trials were announced: Yes, low-dose aspirin had positive effects on cardiovascular health of the subjects in the clinical trials. Madison Avenue produced television ads about the positive benefits of low-dose aspirin (think baby aspirin). However, the excitement surrounding the trials began to temper when other researchers asked questions about the generalizability of the study. Since women and men from minority groups did not participate in the clinical trials, how did the researchers know that aspirin provided the same protections for the nonparticipants as it did for the study's participants? Yes, low-dose aspirin worked for most healthy white males, but what evidence from the study revealed that aspirin would do the same for the groups not included in the original trials, including young white males and white males with preexisting conditions?

There was nothing sinister about the clinical trials or the researchers. Perhaps it was that some of the world's best medical research minds had not considered the physiological/biological differences between the white men in the study and the nonwhite men and women of all races who were omitted, although it does appear they considered the body of white males who were eliminated from the study. Generalizability was not possible, and the same positive results could not be assured in women and minority men. It could also have been that the homogeneity of AMA's membership proved a ready population for the study—a legitimate shortcut. Later clinical trials with women (Ridker et al., 2005) and African Americans (Fernandez-Jimenez, Wang, Fuster, & Blot, 2019; Van't Hof et al., 2019) revealed that aspirin was less effective in preventing cardiovascular diseases than for those in the original Physicians' study. (Although among women there were different benefits.) Studies of aspirin use and its effectiveness among Asian (Rosenberg, 2019) and Hispanic/Latino populations (Qato et al., 2016) depended on factors such as body-weight mass; their specific ethnicity, for example, Japanese or Thai descent or Mexican or Dominican descent; and their levels of health care coverage (health care coverage and living in the Southern United States influenced the important findings in the study of African Americans). Lessons learned from major studies with selection biases were revealed in the Covid vaccine trials. Researchers in the original trials (there were more than three vaccine trials, but only the Pfizer, Moderna, and Johnson and Johnson vaccines were given Food and Drug Administration [FDA] emergency authorization) were meticulous in selecting a multiracial, multi-aged population. Johnson and Johnson included in its original trials an international cohort. Among the exceptions in the original trials were pregnant women and teens, who were tested in later trials.

Another area of bias that currently bedevils researchers is in the area of AI. Unintended consequences have appeared in the many of the facial recognition and language programs created in Silicon Valley. Several years ago, Google developed an AI technology called BERT (an homage to the Sesame Street Muppet). BERT was designed to help researchers discover how humans learn to speak and write. It did do what it was designed to do, but it also displayed some unexpected and unpleasant traits—biases toward women and minorities (Metz, 2019). Some speech recognition programs have difficulty with the varieties of English spoken in the world. English is a world language, but the varieties of English dialects spoken in Great Britain are not the same as the varieties of English dialects spoken in the Caribbean, Canada, and the United States. The AI programs were developed based on the researchers who created the algorithms who used "broadcast English" spoken by Brian Williams, Judy Woodruff, or Lester Holt. Again the researchers were not sinister, just not broadly thinking about the multitude of languages/dialects that are influenced by sex, age, and regions from which the speakers come. ALEXA and SIRI may be the now thing, but there are nuances in human speech that other speakers of the same language can discern that even the best speech recognition devices cannot. Undergraduate researchers in teacher education could develop many research projects based on those two AI devices alone, especially since there are machine learning programs in literacy.

Facial recognition software has also had its trials in attempting to identify women of color. Joy Buolamwini, an African American doctoral student at MIT, revealed significant biases in popular facial recognition software while conducting her doctoral research in AI (https://www.media.mit.edu/people/joyab/overview). She could not get a popular facial recognition software program to recognize her dark face until she put on a white mask. Her discoveries have made Buolamwini, an in-demand consultant, trying to address the biases of AI. Her discoveries also highlight the difficulties in actually producing truly objective research. This is not to discourage undergraduate researchers, but to make them aware that biases can undermine even carefully controlled and thoughtful research. Undergraduate researchers must be alert to all possibilities and include in their research a diversity of thoughts and approaches.

Popular Software for Analyzing Qualitative and Quantitative Data

When I analyzed the quantitative data for my dissertation, I used simple statistics—T tests and ANOVA. I had a large set of numerical data generated by the Semantic Differential Scale. I found a statistician who had just acquired a new computer program—**SPSS**—Statistical Package for Social Sciences. In the late 1980s, this software was just being introduced. The program had been developed by IBM for use in the social sciences to analyze large data sets. Since the late 1980s, SPSS has become the most popular software program used by social scientists (Crossman, 2020). Crossman highlights several other software programs that are useful in analyzing quantitative data: Statistical Analysis System (**SAS**), MATLAB, MATA, and NVivo. Each software program provides much-needed assistance when one is attempting to analyze big data. Software programs have also been developed for qualitative data analysis. The NYU Library (https://guides.nyu.edu/QDA/comparison) has an informative comparative guide on the many programs available for qualitative researchers who find themselves immersed in copious amounts of qualitative data (BIGQUAL) such as AMOS.ti and MaxQDA. Undergraduate researchers may never need to use these software programs individually, but there may be times in which their mentors or advisors may need assistance with large data sets comprising either quantitative or qualitative data. Having knowledge of how to use these software programs will always be useful. The more statistically savvy undergraduate researchers are, the better their final research projects will be because of the careful attention given to producing clean and unambiguous data analyses.

Conclusion

Conducting research opens up new worlds to those who engage in it. Undergraduates in teacher education are receptive to conducting original research if they are given a chance to explore different ways of answering old problems or finding answers to problems yet investigated. Gentle guidance and robust mentoring provide the undergraduate teacher/researcher the mettle to explore teaching beyond writing mundane lesson plans and creating splashy bulletin boards. Each step in the research process from problem formation to dissemination fortifies a new researcher's critical thinking capabilities. Being able to analyze data well does more than provide much-needed answers for a research project. Being good at analyzing data means that undergraduate researchers in teacher education have acquired skills in mathematical reasoning and problem-solving, developed an eye for detail, and become informed writers and public speakers prepared to share with peers and mentors the results of well-constructed and well-conducted research studies.

Notes

1 This is a description of the author's doctoral dissertation (Thompson, 1988).
2 Tennessee's high-stakes testing was one of the models for No Child Left Behind (NCLB).
3 I selected the subsample based on my knowledge of the study and the population of participants).
4 A content analysis is a way to turn qualitative data into quantifiable units.
5 A set of rules for calculating and problem solving.

References

Albers, M. J. (2017). Quantitative data analysis—in the graduate curriculum. *Journal of Technical Writing and Communication*, 47(2), 215–233. https://doi.org/10.1177/0047281617692067

Bear, D. R., Invernizzi, M., Templeton, S., & Johnston, F. R. (2012). *Words their way*, 5th ed. New York: Pearson.

Bogdan, R., & Biklen, S. K. (1998). *Qualitative research for education: An introduction to theories and methods*. Boston, MA: Allyn and Bacon, Inc.

Cole, J. (1986). *Magic school bus at the waterworks*. New York: Scholastic.

Crossman, A. (2020, August 27). A review of software tools for quantitative data analysis. Retrieved from https://www.thoughtco.com/quantitative-analysis-software-review-3026539

Fernandez-Jimenez, R., Wang, T. J., Fuster, V., & Blot, W. J. (2019). Low-dose aspirin for primary prevention of cardiovascular disease: Use patterns and impact across race and ethnicity in the Southern Community Cohort Study. *Journal of the American Heart Association*, 8(24), 1–16. https://doi.org/10.1161/JAHA.119.013404

Glaser, B. G., & Strauss, A. L. (1967). *The discovery of grounded theory; strategies for qualitative research*. Chicago, IL: Aldine Press.

Haardörfer, R. (2019). Taking quantitative data analysis out of the Positivist era: Calling for theory-driven data-informed analysis. *Health Education & Behavior*, 46(4), 537–540.

Halliday, M. A. K. (1975). *Learning how to mean: Explorations in the development of language*. London: Hodder Arnold.

Harvard University Medical School & Brigham and Women's Hospital. (1995). Physicians' health study I. Retrieved from https://phs.bwh.harvard.edu/

Metz, C. (2019, November 11). We teach A.I. systems everything, including our biases. *The New York Times*. https://www.nytimes.com/2019/11/11/technology/artificial-intelligence-bias.html?smid=em-share.

Miles, M. B. & Huberman, A. M. (1984). *Qualitative data analysis: A sourcebook of new methods*. Thousand Oaks, CA: Sage

Pannucci, C. J. & Wilkins, E. G. (2010). Identifying and avoiding bias in research. *Plastic Reconstructive Surgery*, 126(2), 619–625. https://doi:10.1097/PRS.0b03e3181de24bc

Qato, D. M., Lee, T. A., Durazo-Arvizu, R., Wu, D., Wilder, J. Reina, S. A., ... Daviglus, M. L. (2016). Statin and aspirin use among Hispanic and Latino adults at high cardiovascular risk: Findings from the Hispanic Community Health Study/Study of Latinos. *Journal of the American Heart Association*, 5(4), 1–11. https://doi.org/10.1161/JAHA.115.002905

Ridker, P., Cook, N., Lee, I., Gordon, D., Gaziano, J. M., Manson, J. E., ... Buring, J. E. (2005). A randomized trial of low-dose aspirin in the primary prevention of cardiovascular disease in women. *The New England Journal of Medicine, 14*(7), 1293–1304. https://doi.org/10.1016/j.accreview.2005.06.025

Rosenberg, K. (2019). Caution regarding low-dose aspirin for primary prevention of cardiovascular events. *AJN, American Journal of Nursing, 119*(8), 49. https://doi.org/10.1097/01.naj.0000577440.62103.d9

Samuels, P. (2020). A really simple guide to quantitative data analysis. https://www.researchgate.net/publication/340838762

Schoonenboom, J. & Johnson, R. B. (2017). How to construct a mixed methods research design. *Kolner Zeitschrift fur Soziologie und Sozialpsychologie, 69*(Suppl. 2), 107–131. https://doi.org/10.1007/s11577-017-0454-1

Thompson, D.L. (1988). *The influence of educator's attitudes toward a state mandated basic skills test on their use of its objectives/results in planning and implementing reading instruction.* Doctoral dissertation, The Ohio State University. https://www.proquest.com/dissertations-theses/influence-educators-attitudes-toward-state/docview/58179762/se-2?accountid=10216

Van't Hof, J. R., Duval, S., Misialek, J. R., Oldenburg, N. C., Jones, C., Eder, M., ... Luepker, R. V. (2019). Aspirin use for cardiovascular disease prevention in an African American population: Prevalence and associations with health behavior beliefs. *Journal of Community Health, 44*(3), 561–568. https://doi.org/10.1007/s10900-019-00646-5

8 Building a Research Community with Peers, Near-Peers, and Experienced Mentors

Catherine L. Packer-Williams

A critical component of a high-impact undergraduate research (UR) experience for preservice teachers that yields multifaceted positive outcomes is effective mentoring (Haegar et al., 2020; Lopatto, 2010). Undergraduates do not develop research skills in isolation (Boysen et al., 2020). Mentors play a significant role in planning the overall research experience, including providing scaffolded research opportunities where the mentor serves as a supportive safety net for the student as the student gains increasing responsibility for meaningful research tasks (Boysen et al., 2020; Brown et al., 2009; Shanahan et al., 2015); fostering increasing independence; encouraging collegiality; promoting the development of research knowledge, skills, and habits of mind; and modeling professional identity development (Shanahan et al., 2015). Therefore, it is critically important for student researchers in teacher education and related programs to gain knowledge and skills related to building a successful relationship with research mentors and maximizing the mentoring experience (Haegar et al., 2020; Packer, 2006).

The mentoring of emerging researchers can occur simultaneously or individually through peers, near-peers, or, traditionally, with experienced research faculty, staff, or community partners. A successful facet of the mentoring process is the opportunity for the undergraduate to become an active member of a team of researchers. This team structure can take many forms but traditionally includes undergraduates with the same level of research inexperience (Trujillo et al., 2015), near-peers or more experienced students in the research group who have the formal or informal responsibility of teaching and supporting other students in the groups (Trujillo et al., 2015), and an experienced researcher who may be in the role of a graduate student, post-doc, faculty member, or community stakeholder. The experienced researcher serves as the resident expert who teaches through modeling, coaching, and providing valuable feedback to researchers in training. For research mentees to be the active constructors of a research community and to access its resources, it is imperative to learn how to successfully navigate this constellation of relationships within the research group.

DOI: 10.4324/9781003226475-8

Students–as–Partners (SaP) Model

The historical view of mentees as clay that get molded and shaped by their experienced mentors has been replaced by a more egalitarian and contemporary view that describes mentees as active participants who equally help to shape the mentoring relationship (Lopatto, 2010). The Student-as-Partners (SaP) model advocates for students playing an active role in their learning and exchange of knowledge (Healey et al., 2016). SaP models are process-oriented rather than driven by specific outcomes and re-envision students as active collaborators in teaching, learning, and research experiences (Mercer-Mapstone et al., 2017). Using this more contemporary view as a framework, emerging researchers take equal ownership of the learning through a research mentoring relationship "that is underpinned by partnership principles of respect, reciprocity, and shared responsibility" (Cook-Sather & Felten, 2017).

Guided by the SaP framework, undergraduate research mentees hold equal power in the mentoring relationship. Therefore, while viewing yourself as a partner in the mentoring relationship, you are encouraged to bring your passion, vision, and enthusiasm to the research community as you learn to translate discovery to improved pedagogical practice. It is important to proactively embrace the power you have to build and benefit from the research community with peers, near-peers, and experienced mentors. Building and actively participating in such research communities is an invaluable personal and professional investment for you as an emerging researcher. Keeping these principles in mind, this chapter shares strategies and techniques that will serve to activate and exercise the creative ability for undergraduate researchers in teacher education and education-related programs to take reasoned risks, build nodes for your research networks, communicate your needs effectively, and fearlessly negotiate any challenges that present themselves.

The following nine strategies provide emerging researchers in teacher education and related education fields with guidance on how to successfully navigate through the research experience with peers, near-peers, and mentors. By putting the recommended strategies in place, you can learn to use your role as a student-as-partner to maximize the benefits of your participation in a research community.

Strategy 1: Engage in the Practice of Self-Reflection

Engaging in self-reflection is a critical component for preservice teachers to become reflective practitioners. In his seminal work on teacher thinking and reflection, John Dewey (1933) suggested "that substantive reflection requires open-minded and critically rigorous ways of thinking through deep understandings of relationships and connections between and among ideas" (Burbank et al., 2020, p. 15). Undergraduate research programs for preservice teachers help to promote reflective teaching (Evans et al., 2000;

Wubbels & Korthagen, 1990). Teacher education students who participate in undergraduate research have been found to be able to construct their own perceptions of classroom settings, actions, and learning, thus developing a reflective mindset (Nikolov et al., 2020). Learning how to engage in the practice of self-reflection as a student researcher has also been found to have a positive impact on improving reflective practice skills of problem-solving and decision-making (Odhiambo, 2010). Preservice teachers who had opportunities to engage in self-reflection as part of a research community also reported having better teacher-student relationships and higher job satisfaction (Bevevino & Snodgrass, 2000).

Based on these findings, key to increasing the benefits of participating in the research community as an emerging researcher is your level of self-understanding (Zerzan et al., 2009). Therefore, you are encouraged to actively engage in self-reflection to gain awareness of strengths and weaknesses, work and personal styles, blind spots, and trigger points that are needed to develop and manage productive, healthy relationships with peers, near-peers, and mentors. Furthermore, in an effort to capitalize on your membership in a research community, it is important to gain insight into your motivation to engage in research—to identify intrinsic reasons for participation. While extrinsic motivational factors may lead you to feel participating in research activities is a forced or obligatory step to reaching your goals, intrinsic motivation is linked to higher levels of persistence and pride (Stipek, 2002). Intrinsically motivated student researchers are more likely to make connections between research activities and interests outside of the academy, perform beyond minimal requirements, and welcome challenges (Saeed & Zynger, 2012).

Prior to joining a research team, it is important to realize that successful relationships in a research community focus on successful collaborations within the group. The achievement of a sole undergraduate researcher, peer, near-peer, or mentor is not the primary focus. Based on this realization, it is important to clarify the ways in which you can fully contribute to your research community and what personal and professional gains you hope to acquire. Example questions may include, what talents and skills do I have that can best serve my peers, near-peers, and mentors in my research community? What do I need to learn from near-peers to help me progress to the next stage of my educational or professional career? What professional qualities and values do I see in my experienced research mentor that I need to embrace? By answering these questions, students can develop a clearer vision to identify the opportunities the research community can provide.

Strategy 2: Pre-establish Your Goals and Needs as an Emerging Researcher

Using the student-as-partners approach to undergraduate research, you have the power to be in the driver's seat, not the passenger seat, regarding personal and professional goal-setting (Mercer-Mapstone et al., 2017)). By pre-establishing goals in articulate, measurable, observable ways, you will be better able to effectively communicate your needs with the peers, near-peers, and experienced mentors in the research community. Intentionally setting goals prior to engaging in research activities will help you take more control over the research experience in a student-as-partner role. As a student researcher, you are encouraged to let your passion guide the goals you plan to achieve as a member of the research community (Yu & Kuo, 2017). It is not uncommon for students who are new to research to have goals that are ambiguous and too vague. In those cases, taking advantage of the experiences of other peers, near-peers, and experienced mentors can assist in goal-setting activities. You can also engage in proactive, independent goal-setting activities such as exploring websites of similar research labs and participants to expand your knowledge of the types of goal attainment and opportunities that may be achieved by participating in a research community.

As preservice teachers engaged in undergraduate research, you are encouraged to set goals that help to tailor your research experiences as opportunities to expand your knowledge base on how to best help your future students in areas of your specific teaching interests (e.g., mathematics, science, social studies, special education). For example, you may set goals to study the effectiveness of models of instruction, how to improve fluency or proficiency, and how to increase student motivation within your area of teaching interest. You may also choose to set goals outside of your academic specialties to research areas related to school improvement, such as methods of increasing parent involvement, steps to addressing chronic absenteeism, or identifying causes of repeat suspensions. By pre-establishing goals and needs as an emerging researcher, you can better prepare yourself to make a positive impact on the students in your classrooms and overall school communities.

Strategy 3: Be Proactive in Initiating and Participating in Research-Related Experiences

To increase leadership skills, novice researchers can act as active constructors of the research community by initiating and participating in research-related activities that do not require research-related knowledge and skills not yet attained. For example, you can take responsibility for establishing student-led meetings in which you and other students share work-related agendas and task lists and report on progress. Peers and near-peers can serve as accountability partners who offer support and practical advice. Serving in the role of student-as-partner, you can also embrace the power and responsibility you have within the research group by proactively planning research-related experiences such as group writing sessions, field observations, and attending virtual conferences, webinars, trainings, or other opportunities to interact with professionals in the field. You can also take a leadership role by organizing student-led journal clubs to increase confidence in your ability to evaluate research literature. Undergraduate journal clubs provide opportunities for students to gather and discuss research articles and topics related to their research interests; in journal clubs, students engage in research-related activities, such as critically analyzing peer-reviewed, scientific articles; participate in group discussions; and present scientific articles with the purpose of broadening the research perspectives of undergraduates as well as improving student development in applying the scientific process (Sandefur & Gordy, 2016).

You can learn from supporting other emerging researchers from other research communities by attending student research dissemination activities. It is valuable to learn the importance of collegiality and peer-review in a research community. At the heart of being collegial is engaging in positive interactions and communication with others in your professional setting. Being collegial includes being supportive of the research and related work performed by other researchers. Engaging in this form of collegiality may take the form of celebrating the success of a peer's research and seeking to make connections or further relationships with fellow student researchers with similar interests.

Attending fellow student researchers' presentations, roundtable discussions, and poster sessions also provides opportunities for learning skills related to peer-reviewing. You can learn how to identify the strengths as well as weaknesses of a research project or presentation. And, you can practice offering constructive suggestions in a professional manner that is respectful and considerate of fellow undergraduate researchers. You can also practice formulating and asking questions to gain a better understanding of the research presented. These skills will translate to being an academic peer-reviewer and a more experienced researcher.

Strategy 4: Proactively Work to Build Positive Relationships with Peers, Near-Peers, and Established Research Mentors

Using the SaP framework, each member of the research community plays a valuable role in establishing a positive, collaborative team culture. It is important to remember that the people you are working with today may be future research collaborators, co-authors, or needed resources or connections in the future. Upon clarifying and establishing the personal and professional goals each aims to achieve as a member of the research community, every participant, including novice researchers, engages in providing support and encouragement toward helping members reach those expressed goals.

Under the SaP model, every member also has an equal responsibility to model transparency, consistency, and a positive regard for other members. As with any teamwork environment, conflicts can arise. When this occurs, it is important for peers, near-peers, and mentors to remain focused on the pursuit of the common goal. A proactive approach to working to build positive relationships with peers, near-peers, and established research mentors also includes exercising compassion and fairness so that each member's perspectives and efforts are recognized and employing a spirit of commitment to fairness, flexibility, and desire to resolve issues in a fashion that benefits the group.

Strategy 5: Create a Plan to Maintain a Healthy Work-Life Balance

It is not uncommon for undergraduate students to abandon the commitment to a research team and leave behind the personal and professional benefits of remaining an active member. This may be due to a lack of preventative measures taken to assist students in making the transition to a new level of study and the world of research. Students have reported that a work-life balance is difficult to achieve as an active member of a research community (Tan-Wilson & Stamp, 2015). Based on these findings, it is critical to proactively create a plan to maintain a healthy work-life balance as part of the onboarding process or orientation to the research team.

It is important to keep in mind that while engaging in research is a significant opportunity, having other extracurricular activities outside of research are equally important to your overall development. Academic burnout or "the feeling of exhaustion, depersonalization, and reduced personal accomplishment that occurs as a response to emotional and interpersonal stressors" is a significant issue for students and may have an impact on undergraduate researchers (Rahmatpour et al., 2019, p. 201). Burnout can lead to feeling incompetent and not wanting to move forward within the research group or in other academic endeavors (Boada-Grau et al., 2015). It is important to proactively make plans to prevent academic burnout that include making time for activities you enjoy, engaging in campus activities you find meaningful, practicing effective time management skills, and developing and maintaining good working relationships, particularly with those in the research community.

Peers, near-peers, and mentors all play a mutual role in intentionally engaging in "mentoring check-ups" with members of the research group to identify and offer solutions to stressors to prevent burn out. Near-peers and experienced mentors can aid in setting realistic personal and professional goals. In a research community, each member has a responsibility in building a culture that recognizes the importance of student mental health and normalizes sharing when one feels overwhelmed.

Strategy 6: Give and Receive Constructive Feedback with Grace

Giving and receiving constructive feedback is an essential part of learning in a research community. These practices have the power to improve and elevate in a way that helps to not only correct behavior but also strengthen bonds within the research group. It is important to be open to constructive feedback from peers, near-peers, and mentors and to give and accept it gracefully (Lakoski, 2009). Using the SaP model, all members of the team are equal and have the power to share feedback. How a team member handles the power to give feedback as well as receive it may illustrate the member's ability to engage in self-reflection and show insight into their behavior and commitment to the success of the group. Therefore, knowing how to give and accept constructive criticism is essential for professional growth. Responding with a defensive disposition may keep you from gaining insight important to your growth as a researcher. In a collaborative research community, peers, near-peers, and senior mentors can all play a role in helping to provide opportunities for growth based on the feedback.

Furthermore, as a preservice teacher who engages in undergraduate research activities, you should be highly cognizant of the fact that having work evaluated and receiving constructive feedback is a routine part of the profession. Therefore, when receiving feedback from a peer, near-peer, or senior member of the research community, it is imperative to listen for understanding and perspective-taking. It may also be important to ask questions and for examples to confirm understanding of the feedback. Keep in mind that refraining from engaging in a defensive stance does not mean acceptance of blame or responsibility if it is believed there is a discrepancy. Instead, it reflects a willingness to be open to learning and participating in a feedback loop. When constructive feedback is accepted, it is important to demonstrate a commitment to your personal and professional development by following up with positive action. This is a desirable characteristic for educators, researchers, and educators as researchers. To that end, when you view yourself as a partner, it is understood that you do not have to rely solely on peers, near-peers, and experienced mentors to offer constructive feedback. Instead, using the SaP model, you can take the initiative to solicit feedback or advice, as well as personally reflect on your performance. Accepting feedback or advice with grace is a hallmark of professionalism and may lead to more effective practice in the field.

Strategy 7: Remember Your Power Within the Research Community

When you understand that you are an equal partner in the research community, it is important to put that power to use through engaging in self-advocacy. Incorporating self-advocacy can demonstrate dedication to professional development as a researcher and educator. In order for you to meet your established goals, you need to embrace your power in the student-as-partner role and advocate for support that may be needed from peers, near-peers, and experienced mentors. Specifically, as a preservice teacher who engages in undergraduate research, you are encouraged to embrace the SaP model in order to capitalize on the opportunity to gain valuable experiences as part of the research community (Moore, 2015). Tips for putting the SaP model into practice include proactively stating interests to the research mentor regarding pursuing concrete outcomes, such as conference presentations, research publications, teaching experience, or preparation for graduate studies.

When you recognize your power as a partner, you may be more willing to engage in intellectual risk-taking, defined as "engaging in adaptive learning behaviors, sharing tentative ideas, asking questions, attempting to do and learn new things that place the learner at risk of making mistakes or appearing less competent than others" (Beghetto, 2009, p. 210). By embracing the power that comes with the SaP model, the fear of making a mistake will be minimized. A student-as-partner perceives risks as challenging opportunities. You do not have to fear making an error because the support provided by peers, near-peers, and mentors has been established.

Strategy 8: Collaboratively and Actively Participate in Making the Lab/Practica/Student-Teaching Climate Healthy and Supportive

Unfortunately, research indicates that despite the rewarding outcomes of participating in undergraduate research, 50 percent of students actively contemplate leaving their research experience (Cooper et al., 2019). Of those undergraduate researchers who considered leaving, over half eventually decide to leave their research community prematurely (Cooper et al., 2019). While a number of factors may play a role in students' waning persistence to continue research activities, the most commonly reported factor is the climate of the research team. Specifically, students tend to leave research opportunities when they feel excluded, experience a lack of social support and negative interactions, and/or fairness within their research community (Cooper et al., 2017; Thiry et al., 2011).

These findings point to the critical need of peers, near-peers, and experienced mentors to individually and collectively play a role in creating a healthy and supportive climate in the research environment. This can be done through proactively developing a set of shared values, goals, and expectations for all members of the research community. Using the SaP model as a framework, you as a student researcher, along with your mentors and senior research team members, are encouraged to develop a positive mission statement that outlines the goals and demonstrated behaviors that are expected to exemplify not only the commitment to conducting and disseminating quality research but also a commitment to fostering a supportive, psychologically safe, and empowering research group or lab climate.

Peers, near-peers, and experienced mentors need to be equally committed to building and maintaining a high-functioning, supportive research environment that fosters a sense of belonging, respect, empowerment, positive reinforcement, and a good work-life balance. As an undergraduate researcher, you can accomplish this by proactively engaging in open and honest communication about your experiences in the research environment; cooperating with and supporting peers, near-peers, and mentors; acknowledging and appreciating assistance and opportunities provided; embracing the change and ambiguity that often accompany conducting research; and remembering that you are responsible for prioritizing and communicating your mental health needs.

Strategy 9: When Necessary, Move on from the Research Community without Burning Bridges

Participation in a research team should be a rewarding experience that brings a balance of challenge and support. There are times when undergraduate researchers find that the current research team is not a good fit (Boysen et al., 2020). This may be due to a change of interests, mismatch of work or communication style, or unmet expectations for mentoring. When this occurs, it is critical to not assign fault or blame to members of the research community or burn bridges as a professional strategy (Lakoski, 2009). Instead, you are encouraged to take responsibility by recognizing your power in the research community and focusing your energy on reviewing and revising your goals and clarifying your expectations for a new mentor and research community. By recognizing your responsibility in a SaP model, you are advised to represent yourself as a person of integrity who holds the value of mutual respect for all members of the research team. By putting the first seven strategies to use, such as engaging in self-reflection, clarifying goals, and remaining open to giving and receiving constructive criticism, and proactively building positive relationships, many of the pitfalls that lead to prematurely leaving a research community can be avoided.

Conclusion

Participation in undergraduate research has been proven to have long-lasting, high-impact results for emerging researchers. To gain the maximum benefit from being part of a research community, you are encouraged to embrace the concept of student-as-partner, in which you are an active constructor of your research community. In this model, you sit in the driver's seat, not the passenger's, as you engage in activities to help develop leadership and research skills. By utilizing the nine suggested strategies as tools to embrace power and responsibility as a student-as-partner, you can actively and effectively play a role in building a research community, and the joys and rewards of undergraduate research can be attained.

References

Beghetto, R. A. (2009). Correlates of intellectual risk taking in elementary school science. *Journal of Research in Science Teaching, 46*(2), 210–223.

Bevevino, M. M., & Snodgrass, M. D. (2000). Action research in the classroom: Increasing the comfort zone for teachers. *The Clearing House, 73*(5), 254–258.

Boada-Grau, J., Merino-Tejedor, E., Sánchez-García, J. C., Prizmic-Kuzmica, A. J., & Vigil-Colet, A. (2015). Adaptation and psychometric properties of the SBI-U scale for Academic Burnout in university students. *Anales de Psicología/ Annals of Psychology, 31*(1), 290–297.

Boysen, G., Sawhney, M., Naufel, K., Wood, S., Flora, K., Hill, J., & Scisco, J. (2020). Mentorship of undergraduate research experiences: Best practices, learning goals, and an assessment rubric. *Scholarship of Teaching and Learning in Psychology, 6*(3), 212–224. https://doi.org/10.1037/stl0000219

Brown, R. T., Daly, B. P., & Leong, F. T. L. (2009). Mentoring in research: A developmental approach. *Professional Psychology: Research and Practice, 40*, 306–313. http://dx.doi.org/10.1037/a0011996

Burbank et al., (2020). Montessori education and a neighborhood school: A case study of two early childhood education classrooms. *Journal of Montessori Research 6*(1), 1–18. http://dx.doi.org/10.17161/jomr.v6i1.8539

Cook-Sather, A., & Felten, P. (2017). Ethics of academic leadership: Guiding learning and teaching. In F. Su & M. Wood (Eds.), *Cosmopolitan perspectives on academic leadership in higher education* (pp. 175–191). London: Bloomsbury.

Cooper, K. M., Ashley, M., & Brownell, S. E. (2017). Using expectancy value theory as a framework to reduce student resistance to active learning: A proof of concept. *Journal of Microbiology & Biology Education, 18*(2), 18.2.32. https://doi.org/10.1128/jmbe.v18i2.1289

Cooper, K. M., Gin, L. E., Akeeh, B., Clark, C. E., Hunter, J. S., Roderick, T. B., Elliott, D. B., Gutierrez, L. A., Mello, R. M., Pfeiffer, L. D., Scott, R. A., Arellano, D., Ramirez, D., Valdez, E. M., Vargas, C., Velarde, K., Zheng, Y., & Brownell, S. E. (2019). Factors that predict life sciences student persistence in undergraduate research experiences. *PLoS One, 14*(8), e0220186. https://doi.org/10.1371/journal.pone.0220186

Dewey, J. (1933). *How we think: A restatement of the relation of reflective thinking to the educative process.* Boston, MA: D. C. Heath & Co Publishers.

Evans, M., Lomax, O., & Morgan, H. (2000). Closing the circle: Action research partnerships towards better learning and teaching in schools. *Cambridge Journal of Education, 30*(3), 405–419.

Haeger, H., Banks, J. E., Smith, C., & Armstrong-Land, M. (2020). What we know and what we need to know about undergraduate research. *Scholarship and Practice of Undergraduate Research, 3*(4), 62–69.

Healey, M., Flint, A., & Harrington, K. (2016). Students as partners: Reflections on a conceptual model. *Teaching and Learning Inquiry, 4*(2). http://dx.doi.org/10.20343/teachlearninqu.4.2.3

Lakoski, J. (2009). The top 10 tips to maximize your mentoring. Sciencemag.org. https://www.sciencemag.org/careers/2009/08/top-10-tips-maximize-your-mentoring

Lopatto, D. (2010). Undergraduate research as a high-impact student experience. *Peer Review, 12*(2), 1–11

Mercer-Mapstone, L., Dvorakova, S. L., Matthews, K. E., Abbot, S., Cheng, B., Felten, P., Knorr, K., Marquis, E., Shammas, R., & Swaim, K. (2017). A systematic literature review of students as partners in higher education. *International Journal for Students as Partners, 1*(1). https://doi.org/10.15173/ijsap.v1i1.3119

Moore, J. L. (2015, August 25). Students' tips for future undergraduate researchers. https://www.centerforengagedlearning.org/students-tips-for-future-undergraduate-researchers/

Nikolov, F., Saunders, C., & Schaumburg, H. (2020). Pre-service teachers on their way to becoming reflective practitioners: The relevance of freedom of choice in research-based learning. *Scholarship and Practice of Undergraduate Research, 3*(4), 46–54.

Odhiambo, E. (2010). Classroom research: A tool for preparing pre-service teachers to become reflective practitioners. *Journal of Instructional Pedagogies, 4*, 1–14.

Packer, C. L. (2006). *An investigation of life-skills development, racial/ethnic identity, self-esteem, and self-efficacy in high achieving undergraduates of color.* [Doctoral dissertation, University of Georgia]. https://getd.libs.uga.edu/pdfs/packer_catherine_l_200608_phd.pdf

Rahmatpour, P., Chehrzad, M., Ghanbari, A., & Sadat-Ebrahimi, S. R. (2019). Academic burnout as an educational complication and promotion barrier among undergraduate students: A cross-sectional study. *Journal of Education and Health Promotion, 8*, 201. https://doi.org/10.4103/jehp.jehp_165_19

Saeed, S., & Zynger, D. (2012). How motivation influences student engagement: A qualitative case study. *Journal of Education and Learning, 1*(2), 252–267.

Sandefur, C. I., & Gordy, C. (2016). Undergraduate journal club as an intervention to improve student development in applying the scientific process. *Journal of College Science Teaching, 45*(4), 52–58.

Shanahan, J. O., Ackley-Holbrook, E., Hall, E., Stewart, K., & Walkington, H. (2015). Ten salient practices of undergraduate research mentors: A review of the literature. *Mentoring & Tutoring: Partnership in Learning, 23*, 359–376. http://dx.doi.org/10.1080/13611267.2015.1126162

Stipek, D. (2002). *Motivation to learn: Integrating theory and practice* (4th ed.). London: A Pearson Education Company.

Tan-Wilson, A., & Stamp, N. (2015). College students' views of work-life balance in stem research careers: Addressing negative preconceptions. *CBE Life Sciences Education, 14*(3), 1–14. https://doi.org/10.1187/cbe.14-11-0210

Thiry, H., Laursen, S. L., & Hunter, A. B. (2011). What experiences help students become scientists? A comparative study of research and other sources of personal and professional gains for STEM undergraduates. *The Journal of Higher Education, 82*(4), 357–388.

Trujillo, G., Aguinaldo, P. G., Anderson, C., Bustamante, J., Gelsinger, D. R., Pastor, M. J., Wright, J., Márquez-Magaña, L., & Riggs, B. (2015). Near-peer

STEM mentoring offers unexpected benefits for mentors from traditionally underrepresented backgrounds. *Perspectives on Undergraduate Research and Mentoring, 4*(1), 1–11.

Wubbels, T., & Korthagen, F. A. J. (1990). The effects of a preservice teacher education program for the preparation of reflective teachers. *Journal of Education for Teaching, 16,* 29–43.

Yu, M., & Kuo, Y. M. (2017). Ten simple rules to make the most out of your undergraduate research career. *PLoS Computational Biology, 13*(5), e1005484. https://doi.org/10.1371/journal.pcbi.1005484

Zerzan, J. T., Hess, R., Schur, E., Phillips, R. S., & Rigotti, N. (2009). Making the most of mentors: A guide for mentees. *Academic Medicine: Journal of the Association of American Medical Colleges, 84*(1), 140–144. https://doi.org/10.1097/ACM.0b013e3181906e8f

9 Report Writing for Undergraduate Research in Teacher Education

Findings and Discussion

Arti Joshi and Jody Eberly

At this point in the research process, data have been collected, analyzed, and presented as results. Translating results into findings and then discussing the findings are the penultimate steps of the research process. Now you are ready to translate/interpret the results relative to answering the research questions, present them concisely and objectively, then discuss them, and offer some interpretation and recommendations. This chapter will explain how to interpret the results so that the findings are uncovered, as well as how to discuss these findings considering the research questions, the relevant literature, and the broader context.

While there are multiple possible approaches to this task (in many research papers findings are combined within the discussion section), a two-step close-reading[1] approach to provide clarity and facilitate a better understanding of these processes, three peer-reviewed research articles, are used to examine how the researchers organized their findings and discussion sections. Close reading is the careful, sustained interpretation of a brief passage of a text for the purpose of uncovering deeper meaning, purpose, style, and structure. For close reading, exemplary texts are generally identified primarily as models for learners in the given circumstances. The three models used here are (a) Cvencek, Meltzoff, and Greenwald's (2011) quantitative research that examines math-gender stereotypes in elementary grades, (b) Amatea and Clark's (2005) qualitative study of school administrators' perceptions of the role of school counselors, and (c) Kim's (2016) qualitative case study that examines children's scientific reasoning as situated within the dialogues and social interactions in a single multigrade second/third-grade classroom. These articles illuminate the different styles that the authors used to accomplish that organization.

In addition, each of these three articles focuses on different fields within education (math education, counselor education, and science education) and use different research designs (quantitative, qualitative) and methodologies (self-reports/tests, structured interviews, and observations in a case study). Throughout subsequent sections in this chapter, extracts from these three articles will be used to highlight and explain the important steps in writing the findings and discussion. It is anticipated the use of

DOI: 10.4324/9781003226475-9

the close-reading approach enables you to visualize and identify how the steps of scientific report writing are accomplished in each of these different types of studies.

Understanding and Reporting the Research Findings

"Research findings" literally refers to uncovering meaning in the results. To begin, focus on the most important and relevant results of the study and assign meaning by critically thinking about implications of the data. Several researchers frame this section in terms of questions that one may ask when approaching the task of writing the findings (Docherty & Smith, 1999)

- What do the results mean?
- Which results are most important and relevant?
- What story do the data tell?
- How well do they answer the research questions?
- Were the hypotheses supported or rejected?
- Which results are irrelevant to the research questions?

The aim/goal here is to identify how the results answer the research questions. Guiding steps to achieving that goal include (a) succinctly restate the research questions and hypotheses (if any); (b) systematically provide evidence of how the results answer each of the questions and substantiate the hypothesis(es), beginning with the most important and or overarching question(s). Commentary on how the results expound (all or any of) the research questions along with patterns or trends evidenced should be included (Dissertation Genius, 2016).

Writing up the findings requires the ability to see the big picture, which makes demands on critically interpreting and analyzing the results. Interpreting the results while considering the research questions in a deductive, logical manner indicates to the reader the importance and utility of the overall research study (Figure 9.1). Therefore, it is important to maintain a clear flow and consistency in presenting the findings. Beginning with each research question and hypothesis (if any), explain how the results help answer each question; in other words, interpreting the results for their meaning helps bring continuity and flow from the previous step of the research. If the study had proposed hypotheses, details of how the results either support or contradict them is necessary.

Articulating findings explicitly and systematically helps the reader understand the meaning behind the results. According to Clemens (2018), where she drew on the analogy of a writing a good story to writing a

Table 9.1 Useful Checklist for Accurate and Focused Writing (Dissertation Genius, 2016; Falavigna et al., 2017; Hess, 2004; McCombes, 2020)

Do's	Don'ts
• Be objective and organized • Provide consistency across sections of research steps • Ensure logic and organization of discussion • Include headings and subheadings • Succinctly summarize the results • Check accuracy of facts and sources • Emphasize contributions /new knowledge • Acknowledge inconsistencies/ discrepancies in findings • Acknowledge limitations of study • Include recommendations and directions for future research • Check for unintentional plagiarism • Demonstrate professionalism in writing • Include complete references	• Overstate findings • Underestimate the value of the findings • Criticize or minimize other research/work • Making unnecessary speculations • Overemphasize limitations • Overgeneralize findings • Jump around ideas • Introduce new findings not mentioned in previous sections • Introduce new literature • Repeat/restate detailed results • Apologize for limitations

scientific paper, the findings should tell the main "plot/climax of the story." However, it is important to avoid the mistake of making this section too lengthy or wordy, which can only make it confusing to read. Table 9.1 provides a checklist for authors to help bring clarity in writing.

Here are some examples from the sample articles described earlier. In their quantitative study assessing math–gender stereotypes in elementary students, Cvencek, Meltzoff, and Greenwald (2011) articulated their findings by first stating their research purpose and then clearly and succinctly summarizing their findings without repeating their data analysis:

In this study of elementary school children, we distinguished between math–gender stereotypes and math self-concepts using both implicit and explicit measures within the same study. The findings confirm that our child IAT (and self-report) procedures are effective in as much as they provide the expected evidence of gender identity. These methods allowed us to uncover two new findings. First, the math–gender stereotype previously found to be pervasive in American samples of adults was found in elementary school children on both implicit and self-report measures. Second, elementary school girls showed a weaker identification with math than boys on both implicit and self-report measures (math self-concept).

(p. 773)

Thus, Cvencek, Meltzoff, and Greenwald (2011) began their findings section by (a) restating their research goals and describing one of their main findings, which confirmed the effectiveness of their implicit (Implicit Association Test [IAT]) and explicit measures (self-reports) in distinguishing math self-concepts and math-gender stereotypes. They followed this up with (b) additional findings that confirmed their second research goal to examine the existence of cultural math stereotypes in elementary-grade children. The researchers also (c) highlighted how math stereotypes played out in girls versus boys in the elementary grades, providing additional relevant detail and depth to their data. *Cvencek, Meltzoff, and Greenwald (2011) used a clear structure of "research goals ⁊ findings" to help their readers gain meaning from their data. Furthermore, in their discussion section, they presented possible explanations of each of their findings.*

Another example of presenting findings can be seen in Kim's (2016) qualitative study in which she explored second- and third-grade children's collective reasoning in science as a social activity. After reminding the reader that her research purpose was to understand "how children reason and develop ideas in collective space," she continued to address the research question by deducing three plausible explanations that are all related to the data set. Kim demonstrated her ability to analyze the findings and interpret their meaning in terms of the bigger construct of children's reasoning in collective spaces:

> This study explored and analyzed the two episodes of children's dialogues in science classrooms. These episodes contain rich dialogue that contributed significantly to the study's broader data set. In short, these two episodes provide useful and viable understandings of how children reason and develop ideas in collective space. Based on the findings and analysis of Case #1 and #2, three educational implications arise: (1) children's reasoning and problem solving is collective and dialogical; (2) the emergence of collective knowledge and consensus is a driving force of problem solving and yet could form a bias to limit exploration on counterclaims and evidence; and (3) scaffolding is challenging in children's collective reasoning and problem-solving process.
>
> (p. 65)

Using a systematic style in summarizing the findings, Amatea and Clark (2005), in their study examining school administrators' perceptions of the role of school counselors, began their findings section by expounding the "main plots," then continued to elaborate and discuss the four preferences they found:

> Our findings are organized and presented as theoretical schema... depicting a typology of four role conceptions organized along three

major dimensions of data: a) valued role activities; b) extent of role specialization; c) style of role coordination.

(p. 20).

The results of our study revealed that this group of school administrators had four distinctively different preferences for the school counselor role. Interestingly, these differing role conceptions parallel the conceptions of the counselor role inherent in the school guidance and counseling program models advocated historically by members of our field.... The results of this study also revealed a distinctive pattern of role preferences favored by administrators at different school levels.

(p. 24)

After succinctly summarizing their findings, Amatea and Clark (2005) further grounded the four roles and patterns of role preferences across school levels (big themes/plots) within the existing literature. Referencing each role and pattern as distinct talking points, they used a methodical writing style to help the readers engage with and discern the meaning from the study's findings.

To summarize: there is no one way of writing the findings. Depending on the nature of the study, the writing style of the author, and the previous structure of the research paper, the findings can be written in different narrative styles. However, that writing must be succinct, clearly connected to the research questions/purpose, and offer clear themes that emerge from the data without repeating or misinterpreting them. This information offers a foundation for the constructing of the discussion section.

Constructing the Discussion Section of the Research Paper

Annesley (2010) stated that the discussion section of a research paper is like the "closing argument in the courtroom" (p. 1671). It is here that one has an opportunity to demonstrate the synthesis and application of the findings as well as their interpretive skills. Clemens (2018) compared the discussion to the "resolution in a story or drama." Ghasemi et al. (2019) and Vieira, Lima, and Mizubuti (2019) indicate that the discussion should be planned as a pyramid, where it begins narrow, by focusing on contextualizing the findings within the broader literature and other research and ending with the contributions the study makes to the field and practice in general. In sum, the structure and the organization of the discussion section are vital to support the validity and importance of the study in addition to the intelligibility of the entire research study. The structure of the discussion section is presented in Figure 9.1.

Thrower (2010) referred to the discussion section as "having a similar purpose to a satellite navigation unit (SatNav); the discussion should lead

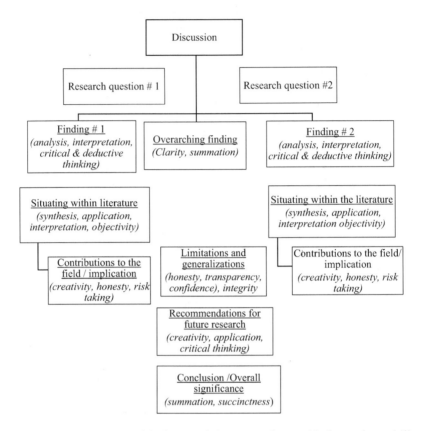

Figure 9.1 Organization of findings and discussion along with demands on skills of authors.

the reader on a logical path from the results to the conclusions" (p. 2676). The following steps are supported by the following works (Docherty & Smith, 1999; Hess, 2004; Veirra, Lima, & Mizubuti, 2019):

• Interpretations and implications (relevance and significance of study) and contributions to the field (connection and comparison to the literature)
• Limitations (extent to which the findings can be generalized)
• Summary/conclusions and recommendations (future research).

In addition, at the beginning of writing and organizing the report, many scholars (Dissertation Genius, 2016; Falavigna et al., 2017; Hess, 2004; Mc-Combes, 2020) remind authors to avoid some common pitfalls and ensure that one has included accurate details. Figure 9.1 describes some of these tips.

Report writing: Implications and contribution to the field. Following the section of reporting the findings, it is necessary to not just explain the results but also scientifically analyze the plausible causality of the findings considering the literature and other research studies. As Ghasemi et al. (2019) stated, "Explanations can be used for clarification, causation, or justification" (p. 6). The main questions to be asked here are as follows:

- What are the possible explanations for the findings?
- How do these findings compare to other research in the field?
- Do the findings support or refute other previous studies?
- How does this study add to the body of knowledge in education?
- What new or different perspectives does this research bring toward education?

This requires diligent, critical skills when making connections between one's research and existing literature and educational practices that have been cited in the introduction or literature review. For example, Kim (2016), in her study examining children's collective reasoning as a social activity in second- and third-grade science classrooms, situated the findings in the context of broader literature in the field and interpreted the findings to make connections to other scholarly work and specific constructs from other literature (such as peer legitimization, which is explained in the quotation below). Using her synthesis skills, Kim confirmed how her findings aligned with previous research:

> Children's reasoning in the social realm supports collective knowledge building and advancement (Hmelo-Silver & Barrows, 2008). In collective decision-making and problem-solving process, the children are challenged when their collective ideas and knowledge are contradicted by counterclaims or evidences, which thus requires them to reexamine or change their claims. This process is also known as peer legitimatization (Berland & Lee, 2012). Previous research has shown that peer legitimization is influenced by the strength of children's beliefs, their goals or expectation for interactions, and their attitudes toward opposing views from peers.
>
> (p. 67)

As illustrated in the examples above, the findings of the study could support, reiterate, elaborate, or contradict other research studies (Vieira, Lima, & Mizubuti, 2019). In any case, the discussion section needs to clearly articulate how the current study adds value to the field/practice in explicit terms. It is essential to contextualize the results in reference to the most relevant studies/practices, citing specific ways in which the present study adds to the existing knowledge and practices or provides alternative perspectives. Cvencek, Meltzoff, and Greenwald (2011) demonstrated that clearly in the following quote, where it is clearly described how their study added value to the existing field by refining the idea of *math self-concept* from other concepts, like general self-esteem identified in previous literature: "The definition of math self-concept used in the current study differentiates children's identification with math from more global beliefs about themselves such as self-esteem (Wigfield & Eccles, 2002)" (p. 774).

Further along in their report, Cvencek, Meltzoff, and Greenwald (2011) articulated how their research augmented and provided new insights into existing practices and knowledge by providing alternative or nuanced interpretations/findings:

> The interesting developmental question is how children's gender identity measured in this way interacts with the culture's prevailing stereotypes about math ability. Two alternatives can be offered based on the current data: (a) stereotypes may be acquired first and influence self-concepts, or (b) early self-concepts may facilitate internalization of cultural stereotypes. The first holds that children who strongly identify with their gender (strong gender identity) are more likely to internalize cultural stereotypes about their gender (math–gender stereotypes), which in turn influences their math self-concepts. Considered from the perspective of girls, this developmental sequence can be expressed as: me = girl; girls, math; therefore me, math. The second alternative proposes that children with a strong gender identity and a given level of self-identification with math (math self-concept) are more likely to generalize or project their own math identification to others of their own gender (math–gender stereotype).
>
> (p. 775)

Cvencek, Meltzoff, and Greenwald (2011) discussed two new propositions based on their findings and logically and clearly proceeded to argue which of the two propositions would hold true based on their own and others' research. That discussion demonstrated the knowledge and mastery of the authors in their research and their interpretive skills regarding their own findings and making connections with existing literature in the field (see Figure 9.1).

Amatea and Clark (2005) contextualized and expanded on the literature regarding perceptions of roles of school counselors when stating the findings across different grade levels of schools:

> The results of this study also revealed a distinctive pattern of role preferences favored by administrators at different school levels. The

collaborative case consultation role seemed to be embraced by more elementary than middle school or high school administrators. This preference of administrators for case consultation parallels the differing preferences of teachers for case consultation reported by Morrison, Walker, Wakefield, and Solberg (1994), whose results depicted elementary teachers preferring a collaborative consultative approach in solving class-room problems while secondary teachers preferred not to seek consultation but instead to work alone or independently.

(p. 24)

Elaborating further in their discussion of the patterns across grade levels of schools, Amatea and Clark (2005) showed how the findings fit in the bigger field of school counselors' roles, thus demonstrating expertise in their field of study.

In addition, it is important to direct the reader's attention to "how the study differs from other similar studies" (Hess, 2004, p. 1239). Presenting such information demands the researcher's creativity and judicious conjectures as to how the study helps discover new perspectives. Cvencek, Meltzoff, and Greenwald (2011), while discussing their findings related to math-gender stereotypes, elaborated on how their study differed from others and contributed to the field in unique ways:

> For example, in one study of stereotypes in elementary grades, Ambady et al. (2001) found that the activation of female identity (e.g., coloring a picture of a girl holding a doll) significantly impeded girls' performance on a subsequent math test. The children in that study did not explicitly report awareness of the American stereotype. We provide a potentially more direct way of measuring whether children have assimilated the American cultural stereotype about girls and math: We tested children's explicit awareness (self-report) of the stereotype that "math is for boys" and the results showed that both boys and girls explicitly subscribe to this view.
>
> (p. 774)

If the results refute the literature and/or established practices, be careful to avoid taking a criticizing tone. Instead, demonstrate depth and breadth in your thinking by providing a broad range of plausible and creative explanations or causes yet maintain objectivity. To this end, it is necessary to use clear, objective language (bias-free) in presenting the arguments and providing all relevant information for the readers (Ghasemi et al., 2019) (see Table 9.1). Also include and comment on any unexpected findings, which might be an indication of the possible limitations inherent in the study.

Report writing: Limitations/scope of study. No study is so comprehensive that it can state its results and claims in definitive terms, as research is inherently limited in its scope. Therefore, researchers acknowledge the limitations in a straightforward and transparent manner. The limitations might arise due to constraints in research design, sample, methodology, or confounding variables (McCombes, 2020). Discussing each of them in depth demonstrates strong ethics and integrity, along with a firm grasp of the methodology and subject matter. For example, if the research design used was a case study, the generalizability is limited. If the sample size was selective and small, it might impact to whom and how the findings might apply. Sometimes, unanticipated variables might have influenced the results, so acknowledging them is important to interpreting the validity and applicability of the findings. Providing reasoning for each limitation helps the reader gain confidence in the author's firm grasp of the research process and further enhances the authenticity of the research findings and utility. Some questions to ask here include the following:

- What are the qualifiers for my conclusions?
- What variables impact the generalizability of the findings?
- How do these limitations impact the quality and/or validity of the findings?
- What aspects of the story cannot be told by the study?
- What questions remained unanswered?

When identifying the limitations of a study/research, it is important to think critically and objectively to identify the inherent variables that would impact the generalizability of the findings. Such a critique requires taking risks and being transparent and vulnerable enough to elaborate on the limitations of the study, without being overly critical or minimizing the findings. This is a fine line to walk to avoid undermining your own work (Table 9.1.) One of the ways this can be done is by reviewing the sample, the method, and/or the instrumentation in the data collection, as each of these can be potential sources of qualifiers for conclusions. Sometimes, unanticipated variables can also impact the generalizability of the findings. Honesty in identifying the limitations provides the reader transparency in the research process and project.

One good example is Amatea and Clark's (2005) articulation of the limitations of their research design and methodology. While they clearly state their design's restrictions, they also offer suggestions for how further meaning could be added to their study by using different design/research methods:

> One obvious limitation of this study is that it used only a small sample of administrators drawn from three school districts in one area of the country. In addition, information about what administrators preferred their school counselor to do was emphasized.... To further understand

and document the nature and prevalence of these role conceptions, additional studies using quantitative measures and larger representative samples need to be conducted.

(pp. 24–25)

Kim (2016), on the other hand, first acknowledged the contributions the study makes and then proceeded to directly explicate the questions that her research did not answer. By doing so, she displayed her objectivity and knowledge about the literature regarding children's scientific thinking:

> The cases in this study demonstrated that children in Grade 2/3 actively participated in inferring, collecting, and evaluating evidence and reached conclusions in their problem solving. Yet there are some areas that this study does not explain. This study does not explain how intuitive and reflective thinking types interact during children's dialogues and how children identify the weakness of intuitive thinking in claim making and explanation in science. Also, this study does not explain how the dynamics of social relationships among children might influence children's evaluation of claims and evidence.
>
> (p. 69)

While this chapter of the book outlines each of the sections as distinct units, it is important to remember that not all papers present them as separate entities. Some researchers may combine limitations with recommendations and/or conclusions with recommendations.

Report writing: Recommendations. Identification of the study's limitations provides opportunities for the researchers to consider follow-up studies using different models, methods, and/or sample(s). Sometimes, the findings might suggest further investigation into examining and explaining confusing or ambiguous results. This section demands the ability to imagine the possibilities of future research and generate ideas and trajectories to further extend the line of research (Dissertation Genius, 2016; Falavigna et al., 2017; Hess, 2004; McCombes, 2020). Here are some questions to ask at this stage:

- What new questions are raised from the current study that are not answered in this paper/report?

- What are other ways one could approach answering the research questions? What other insights might those other approaches provide?

- How can future research expand or provide alternative perspectives on the same topic?

- How does the current research provoke ideas for future research?

For example, Cvencek, Meltzoff, and Greenwald (2011) enumerated ideas for future research in the following way:

> Where do children's stereotypes about academic subjects come from—parents, school, media, peers? Future studies will profit from detailed ethnographic studies following individual children in their every-day lives to document the kind and frequency of input they encounter in the real world from different sources
>
> (Bell, Lewenstein, Shouse, & Feder, 2009, p. 777)

Cvencek, Meltzoff, and Greenwald (2011) demonstrated creativity by expounding on how using a different methodology might provide in-depth insights into the topic. They applied their findings regarding children's math stereotypes to the broader question of the stereotypes' source, thus enriching the field of study.

Based on their findings, Amatea and Clark (2005) proposed ideas for future research to help in generalizing/broadening the knowledge of school counselors' roles and offered implications for designing counselor education programs. They made a clear case, for how their research illustrated possible steps, for improving practice in the field:

> This study brings up important themes and issues for how today's administrators and counselors can best work together to facilitate optimal student development. [...] In addition, this study's findings might serve to initiate a conversation between counselors and administrators about how the changing needs of the school's student body may demand a change on how staff roles are organized in their schools. [...] The findings from this study also have important implications for the design of school counselor preparation programs.
>
> (p. 25)

Report writing: Conclusion. Once the recommendations are outlined, you can formally conclude the writing by summarizing for the reader the final takeaways of the research in a concise way. Typically, the conclusion should not exceed more than a paragraph. Thinking of the conclusion in terms of the following questions may help in writing this section (Ritu, 2014):

• What do I want the readers to take away from the study?

• What new insights the study has contributed to the field?

• What new pathways for future research does the research gleam?

The conclusion, therefore, needs to connect to the opening paragraph of the findings and discussion section, without repeating previous paragraphs. This demands succinctness in summarizing the main takeaways from the research. Articulating in objective and clear words the final statements regarding significance to the field of the study's findings, along with a few ideas for future research, is an effective way to conclude the paper.

Cvencek, Meltzoff, and Greenwald (2011) began their conclusion section with a brief statement about the main takeaway of their research on differences in gender regarding math self-concept. They followed it up with a brief conjecture about how the gender differences might have emerged before they articulated ideas for future research. The authors thus demonstrated their ability to be succinct and identify the study's significance to the field and connections to other related fields:

> In the present research, young girls showed a weaker identification with math than did their male peers. Such gender differences in children's math self-concepts may arise from the early combination of societal influences (cultural stereotypes about gender roles) and intrapersonal cognitive factors (balanced cognitive organization). Future studies will profit from unifying the concepts and experimental tools from developmental science and social psychology.
>
> (p. 777)

Similarly, Amatea and Clark (2005) concluded their report by reminding readers about the main outcomes from their research and their relevance in the field of counselor education.

> This qualitative study of 26 school administrators' conceptions of the school counselor role resulted in a typology of four role conceptions organized along three dimensions: a) valued role activities, b) extent of role specialization, and c) style of role coordination. The four distinctively different school counselor role conceptions that emerged varied by school level and paralleled the conceptions of the counselor role inherent in the school guidance and counseling program models advocated historically by our field.
>
> (p. 26)

The conclusion section demands revisiting the entire study's purpose and findings concisely without repetition, all while reminding the reader of the main benefits of the research study.

Conclusion

Overall, writing the section on findings and discussion can seem like a daunting task. Nevertheless, keeping an organized, systematic format and outline can help you navigate this task with some degree of comfort. Reading many different kinds of research articles on varied topics can help to "train the eye" in identifying different styles and emergent patterns in writing this section. The examples provided in this chapter are just a few ways in which different researchers authored their findings and discussions depending on the type of research and their writing styles.

Note

1 Close reading is the **careful, sustained interpretation of a brief passage of a text**. A close reading emphasizes the single and the particular over the general, effected by close attention to individual words, the syntax, the order in which the sentences unfold ideas, as well as formal structures.

References

Amatea, E. S., & Clark, M. A. (2005). Changing schools, changing counselors: A qualitative study of school administrators' conceptions of the school counselor role. *Professional School Counseling, 9*(1), 2156759X0500900. https://doi.org/10.1177/2156759x0500900101

Annesley, T. M. (2010). The discussion section: Your closing argument. *Clinical Chemistry, 56*(11), 1671–1674. https://doi.org/10.1373/clinchem.2010.155358

Bell, P., Lewenstein, B., Shouse, A. W., & Feder, M. A. (2009). *Learning science in informal environments: People, places, and pursuits.* Washington, DC: National Academies Press.

Clemens, A. (2018, May 21). Writing a page turner: How to tell a story in your scientific paper. Retrieved from https://blogs.lse.ac.uk/impactofsocialsciences/2018/05/21/writing-a-page-turner-how-to-tell-a-story-in-your-scientific-paper/

Cvencek, D., Meltzoff, A. N., & Greenwald, A. G. (2011). Math–gender stereotypes in elementary school children. *Child Development, 82*(3), 766–779. https://doi.org/10.1111/j.1467-8624.2010.01529.x

Dissertation Genius. (2016, November 5). 12 steps to write an effective discussion chapter. Retrieved from https://dissertationgenius.com/12-steps-write-effective-discussion-chapter/

Docherty, M., & Smith, R. (1999). The case for structuring the discussion of scientific papers. *BMJ, 318*(7193), 1224–1225. https://doi.org/10.1136/bmj.318.7193.1224

Falavigna, A., Faoite, D. D., Blauth, M., & Kates, S. (2017). Basic steps to writing a paper: Practice makes perfect. *The Bangkok Medical Journal, 13*, 114–119.

Ghasemi, A., Bahadoran, Z., Mirmiran, P., Hosseinpanah, F., Shiva, N., & Zadeh-Vakili, A. (2019). The principles of biomedical scientific writing: Discussion. *International Journal of Endocrinology and Metabolism, 17*(3), 1. https://doi.org/10.5812/ijem.95415

Hess, D. R. (2004). How to write an effective discussion. *Respiration Care, 49*(10), 1238–1241. https://www.scribbr.com/apa-citation-generator/new/article-journal/ PMID: 15447810.

Kim, M. (2016). Children's reasoning as collective social action through problem solving in grade 2/3 science classrooms. *International Journal of Science Education, 38*(1), 51–72. https://doi.org/10.1080/09500693.2015.1125559

McCombes, S. (2020, October 13). How to write a discussion section. Retrieved from https://www.scribbr.com/dissertation/discussion/

Ritu, N. (2014). How to write a strong discussion in scientific manuscripts. Retrieved from https://www.biosciencewriters.com/How-to-Write-a-Strong-Discussion-in-Scientific-Manuscripts.aspx

Thrower, P. A. (2010). Writing a scientific paper: IV. Results and discussion. *Carbon, 48*(10), 2675–2676. https://doi.org/10.1016/j.carbon.2010.04.041

Wigfield, A., & Eccles, J. S. (2002). *Development of achievement motivation.* San Diego: Academic Press.

10 Report Writing II

Dissemination and Emerging Innovative Approaches

Jody Eberly and Arti Joshi

One of the most important steps in completing a research study is the dissemination of the results. This chapter focuses on the process undergraduates must follow to disperse their research findings to a variety of audiences/stakeholders and in a range of settings. It focuses not only on the academic skills, but also the emotional and behavioral skills, necessary to be successful. Reaching this point in the research process is a commendable feat, but the work is not completed until it has been shared with outside audiences. This is an essential step in the research process not only because the research and findings are important and worthy to share, which is meritorious in its own right, but also because you will gain valuable feedback from the audience hearing or reading about the research, which then can open doors for further research and refinement of ideas. As Edwards (2015) notes, dissemination is a first step toward knowledge translation.

Dissemination of research results must be considered at each step in the research process—from proposal to final product. Upon completion of data analysis, you need to determine which target audience will benefit most from hearing or reading the research results. First, decide who the target audience is and then consider settings in which the research findings can be either shared in a presentation, ranging from classrooms to professional conferences, or a publication, ranging from local newsletters to undergraduate journals, practitioner journals, and education research journals. Another factor to consider is the scholarly level of the research, as that has as much bearing on where and how the research is disseminated as does the target audience. This chapter will examine potential target audiences and then break down the options for dissemination, whether via presentation or publication, for each type of audience.

Dissemination of undergraduate research findings can take place in many forms, from writing papers, articles, or book chapters, to presenting work to groups of people in classes, campus-wide events like a symposium or celebration of student achievement, or at an academic conference. In a group setting, the audience can be small, such as in a seminar class, or large, such as in a national conference, and the written dissemination could reach a multitude of people across the globe. While there are a variety of

DOI: 10.4324/9781003226475-10

considerations regarding how and where to disseminate research, the most critical element is that you do so, and this chapter will walk through the steps in the process.

Bendinskas, Caudill, and Melera (2020) argued that

> student researchers must understand that their original results do not become "contributions" until they are joined to the collective knowledge base, which cannot happen until those results are vetted through professional researchers (via peer review) and made accessible to other scholars (via publication).
>
> (p. 100)

The feedback received as a result of the dissemination process is invaluable and can serve to strengthen your research, writing, and presentation skills. Often, especially in the cases of preparing work for dissemination in peer-reviewed publications, vital feedback through critiques from mentors and/or peers gives you options to improve the work, ultimately adding clarity and strength to the final product and providing the target audience members a better understanding of the entire research project.

The Importance of Teacher Action Research in Education

This chapter is embedded in a book dedicated to undergraduate research in teacher education, highlighting the significant contributions that preservice teacher candidates can make as undergraduate researchers. Sometimes the types of projects completed by preservice teacher candidates are either not considered research or are not considered significant enough to be disseminated to a broader audience beyond the professor who assigned the project. But the question must be asked—was the "project" considered by the professor as research? Or was the project considered just an assignment? Teacher educators must see the research potential in every class assignment. By doing so, the professors help preservice teachers see the research potential in every class assignment. One of the easiest ways to move an assignment from just a project for a grade to actual research is to consider one of the most common vehicles for research in teacher education: action research. Teacher action research conducted by undergraduate researchers can make valuable contributions to the field of education and can be disseminated in a variety of venues. See Table 10.1 alternatives to teacher action research with undergraduate research possibilities and possibilities for varied types of dissemination venues.

What is teacher action research? Cochran-Smith and Lytle (1990) defined teacher action research as the "systematic and intentional inquiry carried out by teachers" (p. 3). Johnson (2012) stated that teacher action research is "the process of studying a real school or classroom situation to

Table 10.1 Beyond Teacher Action Research—Examples of the Research Potential Embedded in Preservice Teacher Education Courses with Multiple Dissemination Possibilities

Courses	Multidisciplinary Research Possibilities
Social studies/science	What conclusions (if any) can be made about the politics of climate change of leading industrial countries by comparing climate change maps to political maps over two decades?
Advanced curriculum/ visual arts	Compare differences in teaching in television comedies with school themes from the 1960s, 1970s, and 1980s to present-day classroom instruction. What do the shows get right? What do they exaggerate? Do any of the shows reflect actual classroom practice? Some suggested shows: "Room 222" (late 1960s), "Welcome Back, Kotter" (early 1970s), "Degrassi Junior High" (late 1980s).
Science/math/history	What contributions from the "Golden Age of Islam" are still used in science and math? Compare the original math or science discoveries to how they have evolved into modern use.
Music	Create and classify the similarities and differences among indigenous instruments used across selected countries of South America and sub-Saharan Africa.
Science/health*	Organic versus conventional fruits and vegetables—A taste test Which are more flavorful, organic or conventional—Bananas, carrots, peaches, mandarins, celery, and gala apples? ***Human subjects—IRB clearance and consent necessary**

understand and improve the quality of actions and instruction" (p. 28). Hong and Lawrence (2011) argued, "Teacher research has been implemented in teacher education programs as a powerful, exploratory tool for teacher candidates to inquire about educational problems and to improve their knowledge of teaching practice" (Hong & Lawrence, 2011, p. 1). What all three of these sources agree on is that teacher action research is something that teachers—and, in turn, preservice teachers—do and should engage in regularly. Students in education typically spend time in clinical placements in schools and complete a semester or more of student teaching. Research completed by undergraduate education students in such placements is indeed teacher research, too. This is the research a teacher or a student teacher does in their own classroom to support instruction, such as looking at the results of a change in room arrangement, trying out a new pedagogical approach or method, or teaching new strategies to children for decoding words or solving math problems.

Manak and Young (2014) suggested the need to "redefine the inquiry-based, scholarly experiences already present in education courses and curricula as undergraduate research" (p. 36). They stressed the importance of recognizing models of undergraduate research that already exist in teacher education programs, such as action research, analysis of archival research, classroom observations informed by a literature review, case studies of particular K–12 students, and curriculum unit and lesson designs, innovative pedagogy, teaching tools, and teaching interventions. Vaughan, Baxley, and Kervin (2017) discussed the utility of action research as integral for future educators to become successful in their classrooms. While action research is rich and valuable, Slobodzian and Pancsofar (2014) addressed the fact that the final product of action research is not often publicly shared in traditional forms, such as conferences or journal articles:

> [I]nstead the product here is judged in light of the changed and improved classroom practices on the part of the pre-service candidates; the success at accomplishing the predetermined goals and objectives for the lesson or the unit the teacher candidate is handling; and the level of knowledge acquired by the students under the teacher candidate's tutelage.
>
> (p. 46)

In a follow-up article, Slobodzian, Pancsofar, Hall, and Peel (2016) elaborated on the collection and analysis of student data in order to improve student outcomes. They highlighted situations in which the focus is heavily on analytic self-reflection in the particular classroom contexts where teacher candidates are working and the research questions are unique to specific situations, such as "How effective is my lesson plan for teaching addition to a class of first graders?" or "How can I support the behavior of this student in my fourth-grade class?" (pp. 42–43). While teacher action research that addresses these types of situation-specific cases may not always meet the rigorous requirements for publication, this is where your faculty mentor and peers add needed support—listening and critiquing the written findings. Your mentor can help you decide to which audience to present your findings and then which journals appeal to the selected audience—researchers or practitioners or both. Observations based on teacher research are also potential content for vlogs, blogs, workshops, newsletters, workshops, and even conferences.

It is therefore important to think broadly in terms of what research is and what might be of interest to a broader audience than the professor or student-teaching supervisor. By considering the research potential in every semester assignment, the professor can guide preservice teachers toward seeing their work as mini-research projects that extend beyond a particular education class. Simply by broadening the dissemination portion of any field assignment from notebooks to be graded to posters and papers to be presented to a broader audience of peers and near-peers, professors can help undergraduates think differently about case studies or field notes or looking at student work completed during the semester. Large three-ring binders of field notes and disparate student artifacts can be converted to poster sessions or paper sessions on looking at student work for all sections of the same class (one audience), presenting the same materials to the cooperating teachers at school placements (another type of audience), or presenting the work to parents in your cooperating teacher's class (a third audience). A mundane assignment has now been converted into research in which the same material can be converted to appeal to three different audiences. Such work deserves to be shared with a broader audience, even if that sharing does not take the form of a peer-reviewed professional journal article or a national conference. Sharing at a more local level is a good way to expose others to the research, and it might be the case that, through becoming visible to others, additional feedback is received for expanding the research in directions not otherwise considered.

Target Audience

As a starting point, consider who would be interested in hearing or reading about the research. Is it classmates or faculty in the department or at the college? Is it practitioners in the field, such as teachers or other

Table 10.2 Target Audience and Mode Dissemination in Education Undergraduate Research

Audience	Dissemination via Oral Presentation	Dissemination via Writing
Classmates/college faculty at one's school	In class; at student celebration of work events; vlogs	College-sponsored student research journal; student newspaper; college, school, or department websites; posters at open houses; blogs
Parents/families/ community	Workshops for families sponsored by schools, PTA, or college; vlogs	School or PTA newsletters; local newspapers aimed at families; blogs
Practitioners—Teachers/ professional staff/ administrative staff	Presentations or workshops at schools; presentations at practitioner conferences at the local, state, national, and international levels; vlogs	Publications in practitioner journals; blogs
Researchers	Conferences at local, state, national, and international levels	Published articles in research journals

professional staff? Is it parents and families? Or is it other researchers in the field of education? How you answer those questions provides direction in terms of how and where to disseminate the research. Table 10.2 provides examples of possible target audiences and corresponding venues for dissemination.

Scholarly Level of Research

Another point to consider is the scholarly level of the research. Not all research is of a level that can be submitted to a research journal or even a practitioner journal, but that does not mean it is not valuable research to share. For example, a small case study or the findings of a new pedagogical strategy implemented in a practicum placement classroom may not be of enough scholarly significance for high-level research journals and conferences. Such research may be better suited to smaller venues, such as within a class, at a professional development workshop for teachers, at a workshop for parents and families held at a local school function such as a PTA meeting, at a school- or college-wide event such as a campus symposium where students showcase their research, or in a journal designed specifically for undergraduate research. As Abbott, Andes, Pattani, and Mabrouk (2020) wrote,

> Recognizing that for a variety of reasons, not every undergraduate research collaboration has the potential to result in high-quality peer-reviewed scholarship, many colleges, universities, and professional associations have developed scholarly journals in which the results of undergraduate research can be published.
>
> (p. 2559)

It is quite an honor for an undergraduate researcher to have their research published in an undergraduate journal as it shows that the student's work is already acceptable for publishing and with further guidance from mentors may subsequently be submitted to professional journals.

In addition to local scholarly journals at the individual college or university level, the *American Journal of Undergraduate Research* is a faculty-reviewed multidisciplinary student-research journal. When choosing an undergraduate journal to submit work to, Bendinskas, Caudill, and Melera (2020) offered this advice:

> In our eyes, there is only one absolutely essential criterion that an undergraduate research journal should meet—peer review by experts in the field. Without the vetting and feedback gained by the review process, authors would be hard-pressed to garner much professional respect for their work, and student researchers would be robbed of a key step in the process of dissemination of scholarly work.
>
> (p. 100)

Therefore, it is an excellent option to consider a peer-reviewed undergraduate research journal as a potential venue for dissemination of the research, whether it's a journal published by your own college or university or a national undergraduate research journal. The peer review that takes place for an undergraduate research journal is not going to be as strenuous as the peer review of a professional academic journal; however, it is still a worthy venue in which to publish undergraduate research.

Shanahan and Young (2018) argued that

> publishing in a peer-reviewed journal is the "gold standard," or most prestigious level, of dissemination of scholarly work. UR [undergraduate research] is not usually considered for such publications unless the work is coauthored with a faculty member, as meeting the standards for such journals usually require expertise in the field that most scholars attain through graduate study and in their academic careers.
>
> (p. 76)

Even seasoned researchers find that their research may not be accepted for publication. Therefore, even if the research is not scholarly enough for a peer-reviewed journal, whether an undergraduate research journal or a professional academic journal, there are other options depending on the target audience and scholarly level of the work. "Achieving publishable results that make a notable disciplinary contribution is not the only standard for successful UR [undergraduate research], nor is it the only reason to disseminate findings" (Shanahan & Young, 2018, p. 69).

Where and How to Disseminate

Once you, the undergraduate researcher, have determined who your audience is and you have carefully analyzed the scholarly level of your work, you are ready to explore the details of where and how to disseminate the research. One model of dissemination outlined by Spronken-Smith et al. (2013) examined the "Exposure" of the research and the "Level of Autonomy" on the part of the undergraduate researcher. With respect to exposure, their framework begins with a continuum from what they termed the "Curricular" level and continues to the highest level of "Beyond Curricular." Their specific levels of exposure are module (class level), department, institution, local, national, and international. With respect to level of autonomy, their continuum extends from the most teacher-directed to the most student-directed. Spronken-Smith et al. provided examples of lower-level exposure and curriculum-based examples, such as journal clubs and in-class poster sessions or oral project presentations. Their examples of great exposure and beyond curricular level include conferences from college level to national and international levels, as well as publications in undergraduate research journals.

Focusing more specifically on the field of education, we created a similar framework (Table 10.2) that examines target audiences and modes of dissemination, from oral presentations to written presentations. At the most local level, similar to the explanations of Spronken-Smith et al. (2013), is the classroom and college level. Oral dissemination at this level can take the form of in-class presentations, college-sponsored celebrations of student achievement events, and vlogs created by the student and sponsoring faculty member. Written dissemination at this level can include publication in a college-sponsored student research journal, student newspapers, or even written blurbs or short articles shared on a college, school, or department website. Other possibilities include posters at open houses and blogs created by students and sponsoring faculty members or mentors.

Moving out from the most local level at the college/university level, research can be shared with the broader community, parents, and families. This can be done orally through workshops for families sponsored by schools, PTAs, or colleges/universities. Vlogs or podcasts aimed at families and the community are another option to share research. Disseminating research to parents, families, and the community can also be accomplished through writing, such as in school or PTA newsletters, blogs, and local newspapers or online websites aimed at families (e.g., www.njfamily.com).

Similarly, teachers and school administrators may be another target audience. As with sharing with parents, families, and the community, sharing orally with teachers and school administrators could take place through presentations and workshops at local schools, vlogs, podcasts, or presentations at local, state, national, and international levels and sharing via writing through publishing in practitioner journals or blogs. Lastly, if the target audience is other researchers, the research can be presented at local, state, national, and international levels, as well as via publishing in research journals.

As shown in Table 10.2, electronic outlets such as vlogs, blogs, and podcasts greatly expand the possibilities of dissemination of research. Jones and Canuel (2013), however, cautioned undergraduate researchers to remember that work disseminated in this manner needs to be of high quality and will likely exist indefinitely online:

> Modern information technology, such as the various electronic publishing mediums previously mentioned, have made it relatively easy for undergraduate students to self-publish their own research findings. When opportunities arise, librarians should try to educate students that when they publish their research on blogs, wikis, and personal websites, or disseminate this research using social media, that this is in fact publishing, and once they do this, it is often in perpetuity, and they should take care when doing this, and therefore treat this type of publishing very seriously. New platforms have made publishing easier, yes, but this also means that much more of what is created

and preserved via online communication can be considered published material. Researchers must be careful and aware of the difficulty of removing our "digital tattoos."

(p. 542)

Benefits of Disseminating Research Findings

While all parts of the research process certainly enhance student learning, from the choice of topic and design of the research to the implementation and the final product, the dissemination of the research to an audience is particularly valuable. Without an audience, the cycle of research is left incomplete and there can be no contribution to the field.

> For all of these reasons—the contributions that can be made to a scholarly community and field of study, the logical completion of the research process, and the higher level of effort and engagement inspired by addressing an audience—sharing the work is an essential aspect of undergraduate research.
>
> (Shanahan & Young, 2018, p. 70)

The Council on Undergraduate Research (2020) described some of the key benefits of undergraduate research in its Mission and Vision statement, including "Enhances student learning through mentoring relationships with faculty"; "provides effective career preparation"; "develops critical thinking, creativity, problem solving, and intellectual independence"; "develops an understanding of research methodology"; and "promotes an innovation-oriented culture" (para. 5). In addition, Abbott et al. (2020) argued that undergraduates who are published authors may find themselves more competitive for graduate school and job searches.

These are all benefits of the dissemination of undergraduate research, but perhaps the greatest benefit of all is the satisfaction of knowing that your research and learning will be shared with a larger audience, thus broadening knowledge of the work and its significance. As Jones and Canuel (2013) stated, "Publishing original research is the last step in the research process. It is important to emphasize to undergraduate students that it really doesn't matter how good a piece of research is if no one ever gets a chance to read it and to use it to inform future scholarship, policies, and/ or decision making" (p. 541).

Voices from the Field—Former Students Talk about Undergraduate Research

Over the year, the authors contacted former undergraduate preservice students to get their insights on undergraduate research. In informal discussions, these former students, who successfully conducted undergraduate research in their preservice education programs, told us what they gained from conducting the research process and disseminating the results. The students provided the following insights:

- Education research is important and an enlightening and rewarding experience for the undergraduate researcher.
- Education research may look different from other forms of research, but it's just as valuable.
- Don't be afraid to participate and seek out opportunities for education undergraduate research.
- There are many benefits to participating in education undergraduate research from both personal and professional perspectives.

The students included personal stories such as the excitement of discovering qualitative research, the pride in co-authoring an article with a professor, and the realization that one can conduct research without goggles and a lab coat.

Advice from Professors

Advice from professors who regularly engage in research with their undergraduates can be a guiding road map through the research process and dissemination of the research. Two professors who regularly support undergraduate students in their research shared their beliefs about the value in disseminating research for the education undergraduate students, how and where they have disseminated research with their education undergraduate researchers, and what factors went into those decisions, as well as what skills they believe education undergraduate researchers are gaining through the dissemination experiences.

With respect to her experience working with education undergraduate researchers, Dr. MinSoo Kim-Bossard (M. Kim-Bossard, personal communication, February 16, 2021) shared how enlightening the experience can be for the education undergraduate researcher to learn more about the broader field of education beyond the college classroom and to see how research is developed and disseminated:

> I think it is an eye-opening experience for the undergraduate researcher, as well as people who attend the conference.... Whether or not undergraduate researchers go into higher education (e.g. attending graduate school), I think it is great for them to experience how people come together and share about their research in the field. They can see how there is more in the field than what happens day to day in classroom settings.

Similarly, Dr. Lauren Madden (L. Madden, personal communication, February 17, 2021) addressed how the experience of disseminating undergraduate research in education helps provide a larger context to the field of education and where classroom knowledge comes from:

> I think it's important that students see the big scope of what we do as teacher-scholars. We can say "research informs teaching" but when they see it and especially when they see the question they explored fitting into a bigger picture, it helps to really make that connection. We don't teach things "just because" we teach them because they are meaningful areas for exploration.

Both Drs. Kim-Bossard and Madden mentioned disseminating the research they conducted with education undergraduate students in peer-reviewed research journals and practitioner journals, as well as national and international conferences, such as American Educational Research Association, Association of Teacher Educators, Reconceptualizing Early Childhood Education, National Association for Research in Science Teaching, Association for Science Teacher Education, and state conferences and conventions. They noted that many conferences have funding and support for undergraduate researchers. In addition, they mentioned mentoring and sponsoring undergraduate researchers' work at the college-wide events that showcased student work and research.

Regarding the skills that can be honed through the dissemination process, Dr. Kim-Bossard shared that education undergraduate researchers refine not only their presentation skills but also their professional interactions with other researchers in the broader education community:

> Presenting their work in writing and verbally helps with their presentation skills (which is more obvious), but I think it also helps them to know that their work is situated in context—people learn about it, ask them questions, want to talk with them, etc. It helps establish a sense of community.

Similarly, Dr. Madden stressed the knowledge that education researchers gain by seeing their research disseminated as part of a larger system of research in the field of education:

> I think it makes the big picture clear for them. They can see where their field is going and what kinds of questions are currently being explored. It helps to know that education isn't some static thing but a growing body of work with lots of moving parts.

Conclusion

Participating in the dissemination of research is a critical final step in the process of conducting research. By this point in the process, much work has already gone into the design, implementation, and analysis of the research. While the last act of disseminating the research brings the current research cycle to a close, at the same time, it opens new doors for future exploration as you share your research, receive feedback, and begin anew, extending and expanding your research into potential new areas and/or broadening your research questions. Research can leave an imprint in the larger body of knowledge of education research and have a positive impact on students, teachers, and schools in the continuous quest for all of them to become more effective and more successful.

References

Abbott, L. E., Andes, A., Pattani, A. C. & Mabrouk, P. A. (2020). Authorship not taught and not caught in undergraduate experiences at a research university. *Science and Engineering Ethics, 26*, 2555–2599.

Bendinskas, K. G., Caudill, L. & Melera, L. A. (2020). The case for undergraduate research journals. *Bulletin of Mathematical Biology, 82*, 100.

Cochran-Smith, M. & Lytle, S. (1990). Research on teaching and teacher research: The issues that divide. *Educational Researcher, 19*(2), 2–11.

Council on Undergraduate Research. (2020). *Mission and vision*. (n.d.). Retrieved from https://www.cur.org/who/organization/mission_and_vision/

Edwards, D. J. (2015). Dissemination of research results: On the path to practice change. *The Canadian Journal of Hospital Pharmacy, 68*(6), 465–469. https://doi.org/10.4212/cjhp.v68i6.1503

Hong, C. E. & Lawrence, S. L. (2011). Action research in teacher education: Classroom inquiry, reflection, and data-driven decision making. *Journal of Inquiry & Action in Education, 4*(2), 1–17.

Johnson, M. (2012). *A short guide to Teacher Action Research*. London: Pearson.

Jones, J. & Canuel, R. (2013). Supporting the dissemination of undergraduate research: An emerging role for academic libraries. ACLR Conference proceedings, April 10–13, 2013, Indianapolis, IN, 538–545.

Manak, J. A. & Young, G. (2014). Incorporating undergraduate research into teacher education: Preparing thoughtful teachers through inquiry-based learning. *CUR Quarterly, 35*(2), 35–38.

Shanahan, J. O. & Young, G. (2018). Dissemination of results. In L.Y. Overby, J. O. Shanahan & G. Young (Eds.). *Undergraduate research in dance: A guide for students* (pp. 68–83). New York: Routledge.

Slobodzian, J. T. & Pancsofar, N. (2014). Integrating undergraduate research into teacher training: Supporting the transition from learner to educator. *CUR Quarterly, 34*(3), 43–47.

Slobodzian, J. T., Pancsofar, N., Hall, M. & Peel, A. (2016). A closer look at the pragmatic model of mentored undergraduate research in a school of education. *CUR Quarterly, 37*(1), 41–45.

Spronken-Smith, R., Brodeur, J., Kajaks, T., Luck, M., Myatt, P., Verburgh, A., Walkington, H. & Wuetherick, B. (2013). Completing the research cycle: A framework for promoting dissemination of undergraduate research and inquiry. *Teaching & Learning Inquiry, 1*(2), 105–118. https://doi.org/10.20343/teachlearninqu.1.2.105

Vaughan, M., Baxley, T. P. & Kervin, C. (2017). Connecting the dots: A scaffolded model for undergraduate research. *National Forum of Teacher Education Journal, 27*(3), 1–12.

11 Toward Excellence in Undergraduate Research in Teacher Education Programs

Practice, Persistence, and Partnerships

Ruth J. Palmer

Recently I chanced on this entry in my teaching journal:

> At the end of the last meeting of my TE sophomore-level adolescent psychology class,[1] a student approached me with this request: Can I please audit this class next semester? I was puzzled. Thinking that there was a problem, I quickly reached for my computer to review the student's semester performance. The student stopped me, and speaking very quickly offered this explanation: "By putting the pieces of our assignments together and now presenting it, ... it was difficult, but I got it.... I finally understand how the class meetings with the practicum allowed me to know and ask questions about adolescents and their learning, and to work with them.... I never considered working in a middle school, but I liked it ... and I want to do this this way again to be sure that I get it altogether.... I want to do it again without the anxiety of the perfection that I brought to the experience.... I will make time for it in my schedule if you would give me that opportunity". The student finally stopped, and I too was lost for words.... The student and I had a longer-than-usual conversation about this course-embedded research experience, adolescence, the practicum, real-life experience (application/transfer or extension of knowledge), and about the academic emotions e.g., anxiety and perfectionism etc.
>
> From Author's Teaching Journal,
> December 2012

The unusually long journal entry was my effort to process the student's request; the entry ended with a long list of action items. I consolidated the list into two interrelated categories: (a) instructional/curriculum design and the practice of teaching and (b) dimensions of student learning. The initial preoccupation with a student's request had morphed into broader

DOI: 10.4324/9781003226475-11

issues about research-based teaching and learning and about structured developmental research opportunities, with research skill mastery and research excellence as their goal. Then and now, these remain challenges for teacher educators and for students enrolled in teacher education (TE) programs.

As undergraduate students/learners in TE programs, you are expected to participate in the pathways built by navigating some essential steps: (a) acquire the component research knowledge, skills and competences, and dispositions (academic and social emotions); (b) acquire related technology and literacy skills (reading, writing thinking, digital skills); (c) learn other skills related to the integration of that knowledge and skills into their learning systems (by exploring, identifying, organizing, and synthesizing ideas and information); (d) be able to assess multiple contexts where integrated knowledge can be used to solve problems (transfer of learning); and (e) generate ways to isolate the higher-level cognitive skills associated with the steps in the research process and transfer them into everyday uses. While teacher educators focus primarily on the program's curricular elements, as students you seek out ways to achieve the above goals while building and navigating your own pathways inside and outside the established curricular structures.

Purpose

This chapter sets out first to identify and illuminate pathways to skills mastery and research excellence as embedded in the explicit or intentional instructional curriculum of TE programs, as well as in extracurricular activities, in the effort to practice, enhance, and extend acquired skills and expand your own knowledge base. While the resulting schematic may only approximate the research opportunities available in current TE curricula, it has the potential as a ready position from which to generate steps toward skills mastery and research awareness.

Significance

Over the past decade, teacher educators independently or collaboratively have used innovative approaches to incorporate research activities into their courses, departments, and schools, including standalone research methods courses and/or course-integrated research experiences. These efforts have brought awareness to work yet to be completed: a systematic, integrative, developmental, and transparent approach to undergraduate research in TE programs. Nevertheless, the significance of this chapter's contribution lies in its intention to motivate TE students as stakeholders in the teaching and learning enterprise, to nurture and augment engaged, self-directed learners and informed, inquiring contributors to the institution-wide change that higher education institutions and colleges have adopted to transform undergraduate education. The benefits of your contributions as a student redound to the advancement of research excellence in TE programs and elevate students' roles as partners in teaching and learning. In addition, it ensures that as TE students, you, like your undergraduate peers in other fields, have ready access to mastery or research excellence.

Toward Research Excellence in TE Programs: A Focus on Skill Development

Generally mapping the progression of research opportunities in TE programs is part of the curriculum transformation led by leadership in Schools/Departments of Education. That the status of that task remains in-progress in some programs does not necessarily obstruct students' contribution to and investment in its evolution. This section reports on the initial results of the analysis of the summary transcript of a focus group of teacher educators ($n = 15$) related to research opportunities in the basic courses of TE programs (Palmer, 2020; Table 11.1).

The program levels used in Column 1 constitute categories that are basic to all TE programs: (a) Pre-clinical, extending across Years 1 and/or 2, and (b) Clinicals, including Years 3 and 4. Column 2, labeled *curricular experiences*, itemizes institutional approved and required course work, while Column 3, *co-curricular*, includes applied course requirements, including early program practicum or internship and a college/university-wide research day or celebration of student achievement (non-graded and sometimes optional). Columns 4 and 5 list *extracurricular* research activities initiated and undertaken by TE students, as practice/rehearsal, integration of research skills, and/or extension of learning beyond the classroom. These extracurricular activities are conducted individually; others are initiated for group work.

Altogether, the curricular, co-curricular, and extracurricular activities serve to advance and reinforce undergraduate TE students' research experiences. So, with the continuing efforts toward the full adoption of a laddered, systematic curriculum transformation in TE programs, there is evidence of students' creative efforts toward skill mastery and research excellence.

This information provides evidence to support the acknowledgment of steps to guide the movement toward research skill mastery and research excellence in TE programs as follows:

Step 1.1. Plan Purposefully: Using a Map of Research Opportunities in TE Program Sequence

At many U.S. colleges and universities, all students in Year 1, including those in TE programs, are expected to participate in a first-year seminar or another first-year experience course. The research-based knowledge

Table 11.1 Curricular, Co-curricular, and Extracurricular Opportunities (Student–Initiated) for Research Practice, Integration, and Application

Teacher Education (TE) Program Stages	Institutionally Supported Research Opportunities in TE Programs		Self-Directed or Independent Learning: Extending Learning Beyond the Classroom	
	2. Curricular Experiences	**3. Co-Curricular Activities Research Focus**	**4. Extracurricular Individual**	**5. Extracurricular with Peers. Near-Peers, Seniors, and Graduate Students and/or Faculty**

Early Experiences Years 1 and 2	• First-year research experiences
	• Initial TE program with standalone research courses and
	
	course-integrated research experiences
		Categories
		• Experiential Learning
		• Community-based learning
		• Service learning
		Field experiences/ practicum
		a Focus on the research process
		  • Case studies
		  • Narrative inquiry
		In-class presentations and participation in celebration of student achievement (optional)
			• **Volunteer toward mentoring**
			  • Faculty-student scholarly collaboration
			• **Self-management**
			  • Journaling (self-monitoring)
			• **Poster presentations**: college-wide celebration of student achievement
				• **Establish study group knowledge building**: reading of the research literature. Annotated bibliographies
				• Explore interdisciplinary research re-practicum experience
				• **Poster presentations**: college-wide celebration of student achievement

(Continued)

Teacher Education (TE) Program Stages	Institutionally Supported Research Opportunities in TE Programs		Self-Directed or Independent Learning: Extending Learning Beyond the Classroom	
	2. Curricular Experiences	3. Co-Curricular Activities Research Focus	4. Extracurricular Individual	5. Extracurricular with Peers. Near-Peers, Seniors, and Graduate Students and/or Faculty
Clinical I	Year 3 Instructional design Field experience—teaching and student learning	**Options** • Instructional design • Instructional research • Instructional materials research • Pedagogical research • Assessment of student learning—case studies Evaluation of materials of instruction	• **Class presentation** on • Research-informed principles for instructional design • Best practices • Critique of materials of instruction • **Launch website** (anticipating Year 4) Elements of classroom practice Analysis of lesson design	• **Reading/discussion group/s** • Becoming a teacher • Classroom management • Learning through research • Teacher identity **Journal club:** reading academic literature regarding instructional design and instructional research (5–7 participants)
Clinical II	Student teaching—local and international	• Instructional planning, evaluation, and assessment • Capstone project and integrated project on teaching/learning experience • Study abroad	• Maximizing **consultation** with cooperating teacher and supervisor/s re-capstone project • **Experimentation**: building *learning through research* into lessons planning	**Weekly meeting and shared reflection** • Assessment of student learning • Becoming a teacher

developed in those courses is framed by institution-selected formats, for example, community-based research,[2] service learning,[3] action research,[4] or other forms of experiential learning[5] (also labeled, *real-life learning experiences* or *learning by doing*). These experiences are often reinforced by information and communication literacy resources and technology supports, for example, LibGuides and Tech support via the institution's Learning Management System (LMS), such as Blackboard or Moodle. Hintz and Genareo (2017) reported on the formation of a learning community as part of the first-year experience and its benefits to students. In addition, colleges and universities have reported on their experiences with seeking to enhance first-year experiences (e.g., Resource Doc_Stengthening the First Year Experience_2018.docx [umich.edu]).

In Year 2, the standard TE school-based practicum is often part of a course-integrated research experience. Furthermore, since TE classrooms have students from multiple disciplines, the research focus is often interdisciplinary, ethnographic, and/or engaging in case studies.

Some students push beyond the co-curricular opportunities to form their own skill-specific collaborative groups (e.g., Journal Clubs, Reading Lunch meetings) to support the understanding of the structure and processes of research.

In Year 3, TE students bring to the Clinical I experience research knowledge and integrated skills and competencies from earlier courses (education and disciplinary). Since this experience focuses on a range of integrated topics, including instructional design, pedagogy, tools and materials of instruction, student learning, and assessment of teaching and learning, research and inquiry often focus on "action research." Action research may involve analyses of student learning, case studies, instructional research, and/or lesson study.[6]

In Year 4, Clinical II may require a capstone project that demonstrates cumulative research knowledge and competencies and serve as a launching pad for students' professional practice. Again, the focus is on teaching and learning, in contexts often different from the Year 3 experience, and with the support of mentors, including a supervising/cooperating teacher, a discipline-specific faculty member, an education faculty member, and/or independent supervisors.

In the co-curricular capstone category, programs may require the completion of a *situational analysis*.[7] The expectation is for students to be able to state a purpose; collect data via site/environs visits; interview instructional leaders, classroom teacher, and students; collect other school/district-specific information; review the research literature related to context-related best practices in teaching and learning; conduct assessment; and write reports.

With their mentors, students' continuing activity (and preoccupation) in the capstone is consultation related to instructional design, student learning, and assessment—activities that contribute to the completion of the capstone project or electronic teaching portfolio.[8] Extracurricular activities at this point are usually limited; they may include online peer group meetings related to the capstone project.

This level of *planning purposefully* provides a broad/global perspective on a program of study and its related focus on research excellence. Students in TE programs can participate in this mapping with the support/collaboration of academic advisors, mentors, and more experienced peers., Partnership on a task like this contributes to building a culture of collaboration and an awareness of research excellence and innovation (Brew, 2013; Brew & Saunders, 2020).

Step 1.2. Plan Judiciously: Map Research Experiences in Education and Disciplinary Courses

This step, like 1.1, is about awareness, planning, self-management, and flexibility in areas that are under your control as a student and related to your academic progress in both professional and disciplinary courses. This bridge-building approach serves well the interdisciplinary field of education and ensures student confidence and capacity when (a) comparing, differentiating, and/or selecting mixed-methods research design, and (b) working and conversing with peers. In addition, this focus on interdisciplinary mapping anticipates the benefits of and success in curricular activities and in the thoughtful design of extracurricular opportunities and clinical courses in which this awareness and practice can better inform instructional design and teaching practice.

In summary, Steps 1.1 and 1.2 emphasize planning decisively and reflectively to identify, understand, practice, and integrate required research knowledge, skills, competencies, and research-related dispositions (Cochran-Smith et al., 2014). The benefits are evident, in that students anticipate, participate, and contribute to the continuing dialogue about the interrelationship among teaching, learning, and undergraduate research in TE, along with issues related to teacher identity and professional practice in K-12 education (Cochran-Smith et al., 2014; Vieira, Flores, Silva, & Almeida, 2019).

Step 2. Plan Strategically: Identify and Utilize Frameworks of Research Skill Development

Any focus on the practice, acquisition, and development of skillsets related to teaching and research need to be aligned with the conceptual structures that provide support for the importance and relevance of the skills themselves. This actuality lends importance to frameworks[9] and, in this context, to frameworks for research skill development (Brew, 2013; Healey & Jenkins, 2009; Willison & O'Regan, 2006)

Table 11.2 Curricular, Co-curricular, and Extracurricular Opportunities (Student-Initiated) for Interdisciplinary Research Practice, Integration, and Application

Teacher Education (TE) Program Stages	Institutionally Supported Research Opportunities in TE Programs *Curricular Experiences*	*Co-curricular Activities Research Focus*	Self-Directed or Independent Learning: Extending Learning Beyond the Classroom *Extracurricular Individual*	*Extracurricular with Peers, Near-Peers, Seniors, and Graduate Students and/or Faculty*

Early experiences Years 1 and 2	• First year research experiences
	• Initial TE program with standalone research courses and Course–integrated research experiences
	Active Participation
		Categories
		• Experiential learning
		• Community-based learning
		• Service learning
		Field experiences/practicum
		a Focus on the research process
		  • Case studies
		  • Narrative inquiry
		In-class presentations and participation in celebration of student achievement (optional)
			• Volunteer toward mentoring
			• Faculty–student scholarly collaboration
			  • **Share in clear articulation of thinking skills**
			• Self-management
			• Journaling (self-monitoring)
			  • **A focus on metacognitive awareness**
			• **Poster presentations**: college-wide celebration of student achievement
			  • Make thinking skill goals transparent
				• Establish study group knowledge building:
				  reading of the research literature. Annotated bibliographies
				  • Set thinking skill objectives
				• Explore interdisciplinary research re-practicum experience
				  • Share in clear articulation of thinking skills
				• Poster presentations: college-wide celebration of student achievement
				  • Make thinking skill goals transparent

(Continued)

Teacher Education (TE) Program Stages	Institutionally Supported Research Opportunities in TE Programs		Self-Directed or Independent Learning: Extending Learning Beyond the Classroom	
	Curricular Experiences	Co-curricular Activities Research Focus	Extracurricular Individual	Extracurricular with Peers, Near-Peers, Seniors, and Graduate Students and/or Faculty

Clinical I	Year 3 instructional design
	Field experience—teaching & student learning
		Options/
		• Instructional design
		• Instructional research
		• Instructional materials research
		• Pedagogical research
		• Assessment of student learning—case studies
		Evaluation of materials of instruction
			• Class presentation on
			  • research-informed principles for instructional design
			  • Set clear thinking skill objectives
			  • best practices
			  • critique of materials of instruction
			• Launch website (anticipating Year 4) elements of classroom practice
				• Reading/discussion group/s
				  • Becoming a teacher
				  • Classroom management
				  • Learning through research
				  • Teacher identity
				Journal club: reading academic literature regarding instructional design and instructional research (5–7 participants)
				• Insert itemize skills necessary to participate fully in these discussions

Clinical II	Student teaching—local & international	• Instructional planning, evaluation, and assessment • Capstone project and integrated project on teaching/learning experience • Study abroad	Analysis of lesson design • Maximizing **consultation** with cooperating teacher and supervisor/s re-capstone project • Insert topic of thinking skills • **Experimentation**: building *learning through research* into lessons planning • **Insert topic of thinking skills**	Weekly meeting and shared reflection • Assessment of student learning • Becoming a teacher • Include topic of thinking skill

Willison and O'Regan's (2006) Research Skill Development (RSD) framework (Appendix A) facilitates faculty work (in terms of its explicit, coherent, incremental, and cyclic development of the skills associated with researching, problem-solving, critical thinking, and clinical reasoning) and students' efforts. However, the framework's cross-table format activates and reinforces students' inclination to self-direction and autonomy. Students can easily locate themselves on the cross-table, where each facet of a research skill is located on the vertical axis, and the levels of student autonomy or help-seeking need are on the horizontal. Furthermore, within each block there is a description of actions/tasks. Example 1 (below) isolates the intersection of Facet 1 of research and Level 1 of the scope of student autonomy. Example 2 isolates the intersection of all the facets of research (from beginning through completion of a research project) by the scope of student autonomy at Level 3, 4, or 5.

Example 1

Facet 1 of Research: *Embark and Clarify*		**Level 1 Scope of Student Autonomy:** *Prescribed/or Closed Research/Inquiry*
Student responds to or initiate direction, clarify and consider contextual issues, for example, ethical, cultural, social (with attention to the content knowledge), plus literacy proficiency, for example, reading, writing, and reasoning	And	Highly structured directions and modeling from educator, that is, the extent to which learner requires support to accomplish the task OR *student recognizes where help is needed and asks*

Example 2

Facets 1–6		**Levels 3, 4, or 5 Scope of Student Autonomy**
Embark and clarify *(initiate the process)* Find and generate *(literature review)* Evaluate and reflect *(literature sources)* Organize and manage *(research method)* Analyze and synthesize *(data analysis)* Communicate and apply *(results and findings plus dissemination)*	And	Scaffolded research Open-ended research Unbounded research

As such, the RSD structure provides guidance for efficient and strategic planning and project management. With thoughtful and strategic use of the RSD framework, the expected outcomes might include (a) setting the foundation and model for a student teacher research execution, (b) generating an oral or poster presentation with reflections for a campus-wide research symposium or celebration of student achievement, and (c) setting the basis for the capstone project and/or a more expansive investigation into teaching and learning.

Step 3. Cultivate Habits of Mind: Align Research Skill Development with High-Level Thinking Skills

Coexisting with skill development in the conduct of research is the acquisition and progressive development of robust and complex thinking skills (Willison, 2019). Together, these skills are at the core of a successful student's academic life and a rewarding academic career. Consequently, it is recommended that as an undergraduate student in TE, you adopt and practice this step early in the program; it reinforces your knowledge base on learning and the integration of knowledge and clarifies the interrelation across procedural and cognitive processes (Lopatto, 2007).

Clarifying meaning and terms. Historically, thinking skills are most often characterized on a continuum of levels: lower levels of thinking skills (LOTS, including knowledge, comprehension, and application), and higher levels of thinking skills (HOTS, including analysis, synthesis, and evaluation) (Anderson & Krathwohl, 2001; Bloom, 1956).[10] See Table 11.3.

However, taxonomies related to thinking skills and/or learning objectives (e.g., Marzano & Kendall, 2007) use varying category labels to reflect the subtlety, refinement, and overlapping categorization of skills, especially in higher-order thinking skills, for example, complex thinking, deep thinking, sophisticated thinking, and systems thinking, as laid out in Figure 11.1.

These categories, separate and together, reflect the most elaborate, intricate, and multidimensional descriptions of thinking skills to which all learners aspire. Complex systems and sophisticated thinking are often used together, and at times interchangeably, to describe the highest levels of thinking skills associated with the research process, although the

Table 11.3 Comparative Taxonomies

	Bloom's Taxonomy, 1956	*Krathwohl et al., 2001*
Low- to High-level Thinking	Evaluation	Create
	Synthesis	Evaluate
	Analysis	Analyze
	Application	Apply
	Comprehension	Understand
	Knowledge	Remember

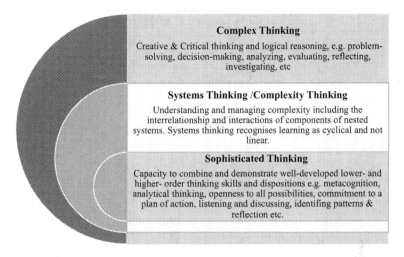

Figure 11.1 Overlapping categories of higher-level thinking skills.

role and importance of the lower-level thinking skills are not underestimated. This information facilitates transfer of knowledge across classes and, in some cases, disciplines.

Complex thinking skills for research excellence. Colleges and universities provide guidance to faculty regarding instructional design to support high-quality teaching and learning. Evidence of this focus and of high-level thinking skills in particular is located in course syllabi goals and objectives and other learning targets of courses (Spronken-Smith et al., 2008). For you as an undergraduate TE student, identifying and mapping the higher-level thinking skills and dispositions associated with research course and related literacy requirements is of great importance in terms of your own goal-setting and engaged learning.

Re-articulation of facets of the RSD framework. Bandaranaike and Willison (2009, 2018) reported on the re-articulation of the research facets (or dimensions of research) expressed in the RSD framework into terminology that best describes high-level thinking skills and complex, sophisticated thinking. Their work was initiated in response to the need to articulate work skill competencies for a specific context and resulted in *The Work Skill Development Framework* (Appendix B).

The Work Skill Development framework demonstrates the applicability of research facets to real-life thinking processes and, as such, serves as

- a way to conceptualize and to foster thinking strategies that are central to research learning excellence and learner autonomy
- a guide and scaffold to the development of student *sophisticated* thinking and of a thinking routine for lifelong learning, and,

- a tool to engage educators in a similar refinement for all disciplines and fields.

Table 11.3 juxtaposes facets of the RSD framework and the Work [thinking] Skill Development framework; its goal is to stimulate students' immediate practice and study of the Work Skill Development framework, as a catalyst to working in TE programs.

Willison (2020) reported further on the efficacy of the Work Skill Development framework's application across educational levels and contexts to enhance and augment human thinking capacities to the highest levels. His research teams and others continue that work. But what this re-articulation does for undergraduate students in TE is to affirm their capacity to initiate and engage in formal and informal faculty-student scholarly conversation regarding this new venture within the context of curricular, co-curricular, and extracurricular activities (Young & Fry, 2012). This then becomes another tool for building the learning community and culture of TE and to push beyond the teaching/learning boundaries in search of mastery and research excellence.

Table 11.4 From Facets of Research Processes to Facets of Work Skill Development

Facets: Research Skill Development (RSD) Framework	Facets: Thinking Skills Development Framework	**Skills and Competencies**
Embark and clarify	Initiative and goal oriented	– Goal oriented – Takes initiative – Adapts to new situations – Identify new opportunities
Find and generate	Resourceful and informed	– Makes informed decisions – Generates and evaluates information – Uses appropriate technology and digital skills
Evaluate and reflect	Learning and reflecting	– Reflects to inform continuous learning – Sensitive to diverse contexts – Embraces inclusivity
Organize and manage	Planning and managing	– Plans, manages tasks efficiently – Organizes self and processes and responsive to needs of others
Analyze and synthesize	Critical reasoning and problem-solving	– Critically analyses and synthesizes to identify problems and patterns – Consolidates strengths – Creates solutions and initiates change
Communicate and apply	Communications and teamwork	– Communicates with professionalism – Demonstrates interpersonal and cultural sensitivity – Attends to ethical, cultural, and social norms

Step 4. Regulate Self: Amplify and Achieve Metacognitive Knowledge and Regulation

As undergraduate students in TE programs, you demonstrate metacognitive awareness related to research skills and thinking competencies when you take on the following work:

- Set goals related to achieving the simultaneous mastery of the research processes and sophisticated thinking capacities (Griffith, Bauml, & Quebec-Fuentes, 2016).
- Articulate and activate plans that are purposeful, judicious, and strategic and establish stepwise processes for self-monitoring and self-evaluation (Griffith et al., 2016).
- Demonstrate *habits of mind* that characterize effective and efficient learning strategies and approaches (Yildiz & Akdağ, 2017).
- Translate failures and disappointments into opportunities for alternative solutions for thinking, writing, rewriting, and communicating effectively and in varying formats.
- Identify and seek partners and collaborators from among the available constellation of mentors, in order to develop a growth mindset orientation in community (Dahlberg et al., 2019; Dweck, 2000).

Metacognition is in fact becoming aware of one's own thought processes, understanding the patterns behind them, and using these capacities to govern learning and thinking actions (Strle, 2012). It manifests in many forms, such as reflecting on one's own ways of thinking and knowing and on when and how to use certain strategies for problem-solving. There are generally two components of metacognition:

1 Knowledge about cognition: knowledge about oneself as a learner and the factors that might impact performance, knowledge about strategies, and knowledge about when and why to use strategies.
2 Regulation of cognition: the monitoring of one's cognition, including planning activities, awareness of comprehension and task performance, and evaluation of the efficacy of monitoring processes and strategies.

The benefits associated with metacognitive knowledge and regulation include the list above and are summarized as follows:

- Enhancing and enriching the learning experience (Pozuelos et al., 2019);
- Contributing to develop independent learners who can control their own learning and learn how to "learn for life" (Lopatto, 2007);
- Providing self-monitoring, which is a step-by-step process of evaluation during the learning process (Bursali & Oz, 2018);

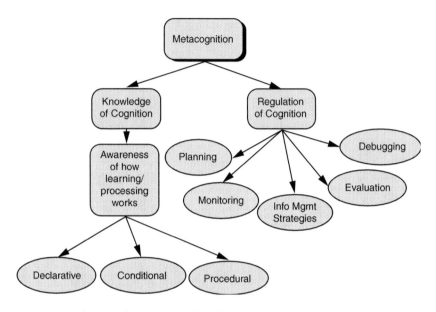

Figure 11.2 Elements of metacognitive knowledge and regulation (adapted by the author from Muijs, D., & Bokhove, C. [2020]. *Metacognition and Self-Regulation: Evidence Review.* London: Education Endowment Foundation). The report is available from: https://educationendowmentfoundation.org.uk/ evidence-summaries/evidence-reviews/. Licensed under CC 4.0.

• Developing higher-level learning and sophisticated problem-solving skills (Dahlberg et al., 2019).

Most significantly, the characteristics of metacognitive abilities can be learned and developed with instruction and practice. These are items you can identify in course syllabi and be aware of in extracurricular adventures and explorations.

Summary and Conclusion

The path to research excellence in a TE program is made by its constituent groups, separately and together, while remaining mindful of its nested position in the complexity of the education enterprise (Cochran-Smith et al., 2014). Each group is expected to enter and stay actively engaged in its continuous transformation and self-delineation by building on the past and anticipating a future, while creating, documenting, and assessing the present to ensure its intersecting and shared purpose with others. This chapter's goal was to invite undergraduate students in TE program to enter and be engaged in "building that path by walking"—in sum, to be partners in this global endeavor (Mercer-Mapstone et al., 2017).

In this chapter, the portal into this undertaking has been framed by a personal commitment to the journey to research excellence established on practice, persistence over time, and collaboration/partnership with your constellation of peers and mentors (Palmer et al., 2015; Walkington, 2015). The initial steps suggested are straightforward and foundational:

#1.1 *Plan Purposefully*: Map research opportunities in the TE Program Sequence

#1.2 *Plan Judiciously*: Map research experiences in education and disciplinary courses

#2 *Act Courageously*: Identify and utilize frameworks of Research Skill Development

#3 *Cultivate Habits of Mind*: Align Research Skill Development with High-Level Thinking Skills

#4 *Regulate Self*: Amplify and Achieve Metacognitive Knowledge and Regulation

These steps enable undergraduate students in TE programs to learn, practice, and gain confidence from and within their many learning communities (Rogoff, 2003) and nurture the dispositions of persistence and collaboration (Hensel, 2012; Rowlett, Blockus, & Larson, 2012). Then, as you proceed in your course of study, you can discover, formulate, and document additional steps in the process which, when replicated and validated, can help you competes with others on the road to research excellence (Jenkin, 2016). Such work contributes to the evolving work of students as partners in teaching and learning and helps to amplify students' capacities as agents of change contributing to the challenging task of integrating teaching, learning, and research in TE (Healey & Jenkins, 2009).

In addition, mastering these steps toward research excellence have the potential to contribute significantly to your professional practice; you will exit your teacher preparation programs well-equipped to be the expert learner/leader/teacher among novice learners. With these capabilities, as a teacher in the initial years of solo practice, you can continue to clarify the linkages across teaching, learning, and research in and through professional development alongside your peers/colleagues (Healey, Flint, & Harrington, 2014). From that position, you can then serve as the capable cooperating teacher-partner for another cadre of TE students.

Postscript: The student who posed the request reported at the beginning of the chapter returned and participated in every class for the semester and was elevated to the position of junior researcher and peer mentor. Currently that student serves as a cooperating teacher for the Clinical II experience.

Notes

1 The course was transformed into an early field experience or practicum and converted into a research experience: tutoring in a school board-approved

after-school learning laboratory, established in an area middle school (a focus on adolescents). Prospective secondary school teachers provided both individual and small-group weekly tutoring to students identified as at risk for school failure by their teachers. It was supported by their parents. Narrative inquiry was best suited for the research approach.

2 Community-based research (CBR) is a **methodological practice that places community partnerships at the forefront**. CBR approaches are marked collaboration. The communities in which the research is taking place are full partners in all stages of the process.

3 Service learning is "a form of experiential education where learning occurs through a cycle of action and reflection as students seek to achieve real objectives for the community and deeper understanding and skills for themselves" (Eyler, 2009, para. 5).

4 Action research is a philosophy and methodology of research generally applied in the social sciences. It seeks transformative change through the simultaneous process of acting and doing research, which are linked together by critical reflection. Kurt Lewin (1944) coined the term "action research."

5 Experiential learning is the process of learning through experience and is more narrowly defined as "learning through reflection on doing." Hands-on learning can be a form of experiential learning but does not necessarily involve students reflecting on their work.

6 A Japanese model of teacher-led research in which a triad of teachers work together to target an identified area for development in their students' learning. Using existing evidence, participants collaboratively research, plan, teach, and observe a series of lessons, using ongoing discussion, reflection, and expert input to track and refine their interventions.

7 Situation analysis is the process of critically evaluating the internal and external conditions that affect an organization, for example, school, which is done prior to a new initiative/project/student teaching. It provides the knowledge to identify the current opportunities and challenges to the teaching experiences. This in turn helps with devising a strategy for moving forward in terms of instructional design, goal-setting, materials of instruction, resources, and desired outcomes.

8 Portfolios provide documented evidence of teaching from a variety of sources and provide context for that evidence, for example, philosophy of teaching, documentation of teaching evidence of student learning, units/lesson plans, professional development—continuing education, reflections, and future direction.

9 A framework is a basic conceptual structure of ideas intended to serve as a support or guide for building a set of processes, tasks, and/or tools that provide guidance for the execution of a project (e.g., research study).

10 Bloom's Taxonomy serves as the basis for additional contributions to the research literature on taxonomies. These include the Structured Observation of Learning Objectives (SOLO) Taxonomy (Biggs & Collin, 1982), Marzano's (1998) taxonomy of learning that integrated three domains/systems: the self-system, which involves student motivation; the metacognitive system, involving goal-setting and planning; and the cognitive system. The New Taxonomy (Marzano & Kendall, 2007) comprehensively and systematically defines a wide variety of skills related to thinking and learning.

References

Anderson, L. W., & Krathwohl, D. R. (2001). *A taxonomy for learning, teaching and assessing: A revision of bloom's taxonomy of educational objectives*. New York: Longman.

Bandaranaike, S., & Willison, J. (2009). Work skill development framework: An innovative assessment for work integrated learning. *Asia-Pacific Journal of Cooperative Education, 16*(3), 223–233.

Bloom, B. S. (1956). *Taxonomy of educational objectives, handbook I: The cognitive domain.* New York: David McKay Co Inc.

Brew, A. (2013). Understanding the scope of undergraduate research: A framework for curricular and pedagogical decision-making. *Higher Education, 66,* 603–618.

Brew, A., & Saunders, C. (2020). Making sense of research-based learning in teacher education. *Teaching and Teacher Education, 87.* Article number 102935.

Bursali, N., & Oz, H. (2018). The role of goal setting in metacognitive awareness as a self-regulatory behavior in foreign language learning. *International Online Journal of Education & Teaching, 5*(3), 662–671.

Cochran-Smith, M., Ell, F., Ludlow, L., Grudnoff, L., & Aitken, G. (2014). The challenge and promise of complexity theory for teacher education research. *Teachers College Record, 116*(5), 1–38.

Dahlberg, C. L., Wiggins, B. L., Lee, S. R., Leaf, D. S., Lily, L. S., Jordt, H., & Johnson, T. J. (2019). A short, course-based research module provides metacognitive benefits in the form of more sophisticated problem solving. *Journal of College Science Teaching, 48*(4), 22–30.

Dweck, C. S. (2000). *Self-theories: Their role in motivation, personality, and development.* East Sussex: Psychology Press.

Eyler, J. (2009). The power of experiential education. *AAC&U Newsletter, 95*(4), 24–31.

Griffith, R., Bauml, M., & Quebec-Fuentes, S. (2016). Promoting metacognitive decision-making in teacher education. *Theory into Practice, 55*(3), 242–249.

Healey, M., Flint, A., & Harrington, K. (2014). *Engagement through partnership: Students as partners in learning and teaching in higher education.* York: HE Academy.

Healey, M., & Jenkins, A. (2009). *Developing undergraduate research and inquiry.* York: Higher Education Academy. http://www.heacademy.ac.uk/assets/York/documents/

Hensel, N. (Ed.). (2012). *Characteristics of Excellence in Undergraduate Research (COEUR).* Washington, DC: Council on Undergraduate Research.

Hintz, K., & Genareo, V. (2017). Suggestions for implementing first-year experience learning communities in teacher education programs. *Learning Communities Research and Practice, 5*(1), Article 2.

Jenkins, A. (2016). *Developing undergraduate research and inquiry. Heslington*: The Higher Education Academy.

Krathwohl, D. R. (2002). A revision of Bloom's taxonomy: An overview. *Theory Into Practice, 41*(4), 212–218. http://www.jstor.org/stable/1477405

Lewin, K. (1944). Constructs in psychology and psychological ecology. *University of Iowa Studies* in *Child Welfare, 20,* 3– 29. Reprinted (in part) in Cartwright, 1951, Chapter 7.

Lopatto, D. (2007). Undergraduate research experiences support science career decisions and active learning. *CBE Life Science Education, 6*(4), 297–306. doi:10.1187/cbe.07-06-0039

Marzano, R. J. (1998). *A theory-based meta-analysis of research on instruction.* Washington, DC: Office of Educational Research and Improvement (ED).

Marzano, R. J. & Kendall, R. J. (2007). *The new taxonomy of educational objectives: Edition 2.* Newbury Park, CA: Corwin Press

Mercer-Mapstone, L., Dvorakova, S. L., Matthews, K. E., Abbot, S., Cheng, B., Felten, P., Knorr, K., Marquis, E., Shammas, R., & Swaim, K. (2017). A systematic literature review of Students as Partners in higher education. *International Journal for Students as Partners*, *1*(1). https://doi.org/10.15173/ijsap.v1i1.3119

Palmer, R. J. (2020). Exploring structured opportunities for research development in teacher education programs (Unpublished manuscript). Faculty Emeritus, The College of New Jersey.

Palmer, R. J., Hunt, A. N., Neal, M., & Wuetherick, B. (2015). Mentoring, undergraduate research, and identity development: A conceptual review and research agenda. *Mentoring and Tutoring 23*(5), 1–16. https://doi.org/10.1080/1 3611267.2015.1126165

Pozuelos, J. P., Combita, L. M., Abundis, A., Paz-Alonso, P. M., Conejero, Á., Guerra, S., & Rueda, M. R. (2019). Metacognitive scaffolding boosts cognitive and neural benefits following executive attention training in children. *Developmental Science*, *22*(2), nk.

Rogoff, B. (2003). *The cultural nature of development*. Oxford: Oxford University Press.

Rowlett, R. S., Blockus, L., & Larson, S. (2012). Characteristics of excellence in undergraduate research (COEUR). In *Characteristics of excellence in undergraduate research (COEUR)* (pp. 2–19). Washington, DC: Council on Undergraduate Research.

Spronken-Smith, R. A., Walker, R., O'Steen, W., Matthews, H., Batchelor, J., & Angelo, T. (2008). *Reconceptualizing inquiry-based learning: Synthesis of findings*. Wellington, NZ: Ako Aotearoa, The National Centre for Tertiary Teaching Excellence.

Strle, T. (2012). Metacognition and decision making: Between first- and third-person perspective. *Interdisciplinary Description of Complex Systems*, *10*(3), 284–297.

Vieira, F., Flores, M. A., Silva, J. L., & Almeida, J. (2019). Understanding and enhancing change in post-Bologna pre-service teacher education: Lessons from experience and research in Portugal, in T. Al Barwani, M. A. Flores, & D. Imig (Eds.) *Leading change in teacher education: Lessons from countries and education leaders around the globe* (pp. 41–57). Milton Park: Routledge.

Walkington, H. (2015). *Students as researchers: Supporting undergraduate research in the disciplines in higher education*. York: Higher Education Academy.

Willison, J. W. (2018). Research skill development spanning higher education: Critiques, curricula and connections. *Journal of University Teaching & Learning Practice*, *15*(4), 1–15.

Willison, J. W. (2019). *The Models of Engaged Learning, connecting sophisticated thinking from early childhood to Ph.D*. Gateway East, Singapore: Springer Briefs in Education.

Willison, J. (2020). *The models of engaged learning and teaching connecting sophisticated thinking from early childhood to PhD*. Gateway East, Singapore: Springer Open.

Willison, J., & O'Regan, K. (2006). *Research skill development framework*. Retrieved from University of Adelaide website: http://www.adelaide.edu.au/rsd/framework/rsd-framework.pdf

Yildiz, H., & Akdağ, M. (2017). The effect of metacognitive strategies on prospective teachers' metacognitive awareness and self-efficacy belief. *Journal of Education and Training Studies*, *5*(12), 30–40.

Young, A., & Fry, J. (2012). Metacognitive awareness and academic achievement in college students. *The Journal of Scholarship of Teaching and Learning*, *8*, 2–16.

Appendix A

Research Skill Development (Willison & O'Regan, 2006)

For a more detailed look, please see: Research Skill Development (adelaide.edu.au)

Table 11.1A Research Skill Development (RSD) Framework

For educators to facilitate the explicit, coherent, incremental, and cyclic development of the skills associated with researching, problem-solving, critical thinking, and cleaning reasoning.

Scope for student Autonomy

	Prescribed research	Bounded research	Scaffolded research	Open-ended research	Unbounded research
Students develop research mindedness when they…	Highly structured directions and modeling from educator prompt researching, in which…	Boundaries set by and limited directions from educator channel researching, in which…	Scaffolds placed by educator shape independent researching, in which…	Students initiate research and this is guided by the educator.	Students determine guidelines for researching that are in accord with discipline or context.
Embark and clarify *What is our purpose?* Students respond to or initiate direction; clarify and consider ethical, cultural, social, and team (ECST) issues.	Curious				
	Students respond to questions/tasks that are directed. Use a provided, structured approach to clarify questions, terms, requirements, expectations, and ECST issues.	Students respond to questions/ tasks with limited options. Choose from several provided structures to clarify questions, requirements, terms, expectations, and ECST issues.	Students respond to broad tasks/ questions given. Choose from a range of provided approaches or structures to clarify requirements, questions, expectations, and ECST issues.	⋆*Students generate questions /aims/hypotheses/ purpose framed within structured guidelines*⋆. Anticipate and prepare for ECST issues.	⋆*Students generate questions/aims/ hypotheses/ purpose based on experience, expertise, and literature.* Delve into and prepare for ECST issues.

(Continued)

Scope for student Autonomy

Find and generate *What do we need?* Students find information and generate data/ideas using appropriate methodology.	Determined	Students collect and record required information/data using a prescribed methodology from a prescribed source in which the information/data are evident.	Students collect and record appropriate information/data using given methodology from predetermined source/s where information/data are not obvious.	Students collect and record appropriate information/data from self-selected sources using one of several provided methodologies.	Students collect and record self-determined information/data choosing an appropriate methodology based on parameters set.	Students collect and record information/data from self-selected sources, choosing or devising an appropriate methodology with self-structured guidelines.
Evaluate and reflect *What do we trust?* Students determine the credibility of sources, information, data, and ideas, and make their own research processes visible.	Disseminating	Students evaluate sources/information/data using simple prescribed criteria to specify credibility and to reflect on and improve the process used.	Students evaluate sources/information/data using a choice of provided criteria to specify credibility and to reflect on and improve processes used.	Students evaluate sources/information/data and the processes to find/generate, using criteria related to the aims of the inquiry to reflect on and improve processes used.	Students evaluate information/data and the inquiry process using self-determined criteria developed within parameters given. Reflect to refine own and others' processes.	Students evaluate information/data and inquiry process rigorously using self-generated criteria based on experience, expertise, and the literature. Reflect to renew own and others' processes.

Organize and manage *How do we arrange?* Students organize information and data to reveal patterns/themes, managing teams and processes.	Harmonizing	Students organize information/data using prescribed structure. Manage linear process provided (with prespecified team roles).	Students organize information/data using a choice of given structures. Manage a process that has alternative possible pathways (and specify team roles).	Students organize information/data using provided guidelines to choose structures. Manage processes (and teams) with multiple possible pathways.	Students organize information/data using self-determined or group-determined structures and manage the processes (including team function) within the parameters set.	Students organize information/data using self-determined or group-determined structures and management processes (including team function).
Analyze and synthesize *What does it mean?* Students analyze information/data critically and synthesize new knowledge to produce coherent individual/team understandings.	Creative	Students interpret given information/data, determine patterns, and synthesize knowledge into prescribed formats. ★*Ask emergent questions of clarification/curiosity*★.	Students analyze trends or themes in several sources of information/data and synthesize to integrate knowledge into provided standard formats. ★*Ask emergent, relevant, and researchable questions*★.	Students analyze trends or themes in information/data and synthesize to fully integrate component parts in structures that are appropriate to task. ★*Ask rigorous, researchable questions based on new understandings*★.	Students analyze information/data and synthesize to fully integrate components, consistent with self-determined parameters. Fill knowledge gaps that are stated by others.	Students analyze and synthesize information/data to generalize or abstract knowledge that addresses self-identified or group-identified gaps in understanding.

(Continued)

Communicate and apply / How do we relate?	Constructive					
Communicate and apply *How do we relate?* Students apply their understanding and discuss, listen, write, perform, respond to feedback, and present processes, knowledge, and implications of research, heeding ECST issues and audience needs.		Students discuss with each other, listen, read, and write to relate their prior and new knowledge to set tasks. Use prescribed language and genre to develop understanding and then demonstrate this to a specified audience. Apply to a similar context the knowledge developed. Follow prompts on ECST issues.	Students use some discipline-specific language and genre to relate their prior and newly developed knowledge to tasks and then to a specified audience. Apply the knowledge developed to several similar contexts and stay within boundaries set for ECST issues.	Students use discipline-specific or other appropriate language and select genres to develop understanding and relate this to an audience chosen from given options. Apply the knowledge developed to different contexts and specify the ECST issues that emerge.	Students choose appropriate language, genre, and performance to extend the knowledge of an audience they have selected. Apply the knowledge developed to diverse contexts and specify ECST issues in initiating, conducting, and communicating.	Students choose appropriate language, genre, and performance to extend the knowledge of a range of audiences. Apply innovatively the knowledge developed to multiple contexts. Probe and specify ECST issues that emerge broadly.
Research is not merely gathering more information and generating more data. Research is engaging in all the above facets time and again	The Research Skill Development (RSD), a conceptual framework for Early Childhood to PhD, by John Willison and Kerry O'Regan, with much trialing by Eleanor Peirce and Mario Ricci. October 2006, revised August 2018. Facets based on: Australian and New Zealand Institute for Information and Literacy (ANZIIL, 2004) and Bloom et al. (1956, 1964) Taxonomies: Perpendicular text reflects learning attitudes. Scope and autonomy inspired by Vygotsky (1980). Extent of synthesis is informed by Structure of the Observed Learning Outcome (SOLO) taxonomy (Biggs & Collin, 1982). ★Framing researchable questions often requires a high degree of guidance and modeling for students and results from their synthesis (Red to Yellow) then initiates their research (Green and Blue). Six facets may be used directly with students as a 'thinking routine' (Ritchhart & Perkins 2008). Resources and articles available at www.rsd.edu.au; email: john.willison@adelaide.edu.au The RSD is the first of the Models of Engaged Learning and Teaching (MELT). www.melt.edu.au					

Appendix B

The Work Skill Development Framework (Bandarinake & Willison, 2018)

For a more detailed look, please see: https://www.adelaide.edu.au/melt/ua/media/42/rsd_24aug18.pdf

Table 11.1B The Work Skill Development Framework

Scope for Student Autonomy

Work skill facets	Prescribed direction *Highly structured directions and guidance from mentor where, the student…*	Bounded direction *Boundaries set by and limited directions from mentor where, the student…*	Scaffolded direction *Demonstrates some independence within provided guidelines, where the student…*	Open-ended *Works independently to innovative with limited guidance, where the student…*	Unbounded *Works within self-determined guidelines appropriate to context, where the student…*
Initiative and goal-oriented *What is my role?* Goal-oriented and takes the initiative to clarify role, adapt to new situations, and identify new opportunities.	Motivated				
	Requires a high degree of guidance to clarify role and adapt to new situations.	Requires some direction to carry out role with an awareness of the opportunities it offers.	Establishes role independently and adapts to situations with minimal guidance.	Motivated to fulfill the potential the role offers by exploring new goals and opportunities in a range of contexts.	Determines future goals and projects which create innovative, strategic outcomes. Regularly exceeds potential.

(Continued)

Resourceful and informed *What do I need?* Makes informed decisions by finding, generating, and evaluating information using appropriate technology and digital skills.	Discerning	Finds required information using prescribed technology with a high degree of structure and guidance.	Interprets affordances of technology for finding and generating information and the skills required to use digital tools with limited direction.	Determines the affordances of technology and applies digital skills for finding, selecting, and generating context-specific information.	Uses a range of technologies and demonstrates adeptness with digital skills and technologies when locating, generating, and evaluating information to make informed decisions.	Effectively and discerningly selects, generates, and evaluates information and data to make strategic decisions and to stay informed.
Learning and reflecting *How do I improve?* Reflects insightfully for continuous learning, encompassing inclusivity in diverse work environments.	Empowering	Requires guidance to develop reflective practices for continuous professional learning that includes understanding inclusivity in diverse work environments.	Demonstrates some behaviors for continuous learning, recognizing the importance of inclusive practices.	Aligns behavior and learning goals with organizational objectives and protocols, and applies inclusivity in diverse work environments.	Evaluates and reflects on learning with a high degree of insight to determine professional learning goals. Is committed to behaviors that foster inclusivity in a diverse workplace.	Evaluates and reflects on behavior and work practices required to achieve a healthy organizational culture, takes responsibility for the intellectual and social development of others.

Planning and management *How do I organize?* Plans, manages, organizes self and processes while being perceptive to managing the needs of others.	Mindful	Requires a high degree of guidance to organize and manage self and processes using prescribed structures.	Manages self and establishes clear project goals and deliverables, with limited guidance.	Plans and monitors processes for organizing and managing self and others within provided guidelines.	Prioritizes time and resources, plans for contingencies while managing and organizing tasks for self and others.	Determines priorities, directs, and articulates strategic vision plans and is perceptive to the needs of others.
Critical reasoning and problem-solving *How do I solve?* Critically analyzes and synthesizes to identify problems, consolidate strengths, create solutions, and initiate necessary change.	Creative	Requires a high degree of guidance to identify and understand known problems that have known solutions.	Follows established protocols to understand and find solutions to known problems with limited direction.	Requires minimal guidance to analyze and synthesize problems, using existing knowledge. Recognizes the impact of bias on enabling solutions.	Applies critical reasoning to independently solve increasingly complex problems as they arise. Finds innovative and considered solutions for successful outcomes.	Applies sophisticated, evidence-based reasoning to solve problems skillfully and creatively. Demonstrates nuanced understanding of implications.

(Continued)

Scope for Student Autonomy

Communication and teamwork *How do I relate?* Communicates with professionalism, interpersonal and cultural sensitivity heeding ethical, cultural social, and team (ECST) dynamics.	Ethical	Follows prescribed structures and organizational protocols to communicate within and outside team environments, guided modeling develops awareness of ECST considerations in the workplace.	Some guidance is required to consider other perspectives, exchange information; communicates ideas between inter-professional teams. Shows awareness of ECST issues.	Demonstrates understanding of team dynamics, contributes effectively to common goals. Communicates assertively and confidently; actively listens to others and adapts to ECST practices.	Demonstrates ability to coordinate and socialize diverse teams, communicates complex information effectively and sensitively, cultivates open communication, provides constructive feedback aligned with ECST practices.	Demonstrates leadership of inter-professional teams in culturally diverse settings; clearly communicates goals to generate and meet strategic outcomes. Leads by example to inculcate ECST practices.

For the explicit and coherent development of student employability skills. Bandaranaike and Willison (2009, 2018). suniti.bandaranaike@jcu.edu.au Revised by Monash University Library, 2019. lynette.torres@monash.edu barbara.yazbeck@monash.edu www.adelaide.edu.au/rsd/melt/www.monash.edu/library/skills/rsd

Index

Note: **Bold** page numbers refer to tables; *italic* page numbers refer to figures and page numbers followed by "n" denote endnotes.

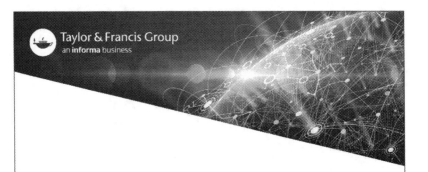

Printed in the United States
by Baker & Taylor Publisher Services